THE ART OF
HALO 5
GUARDIANS

John Liberto

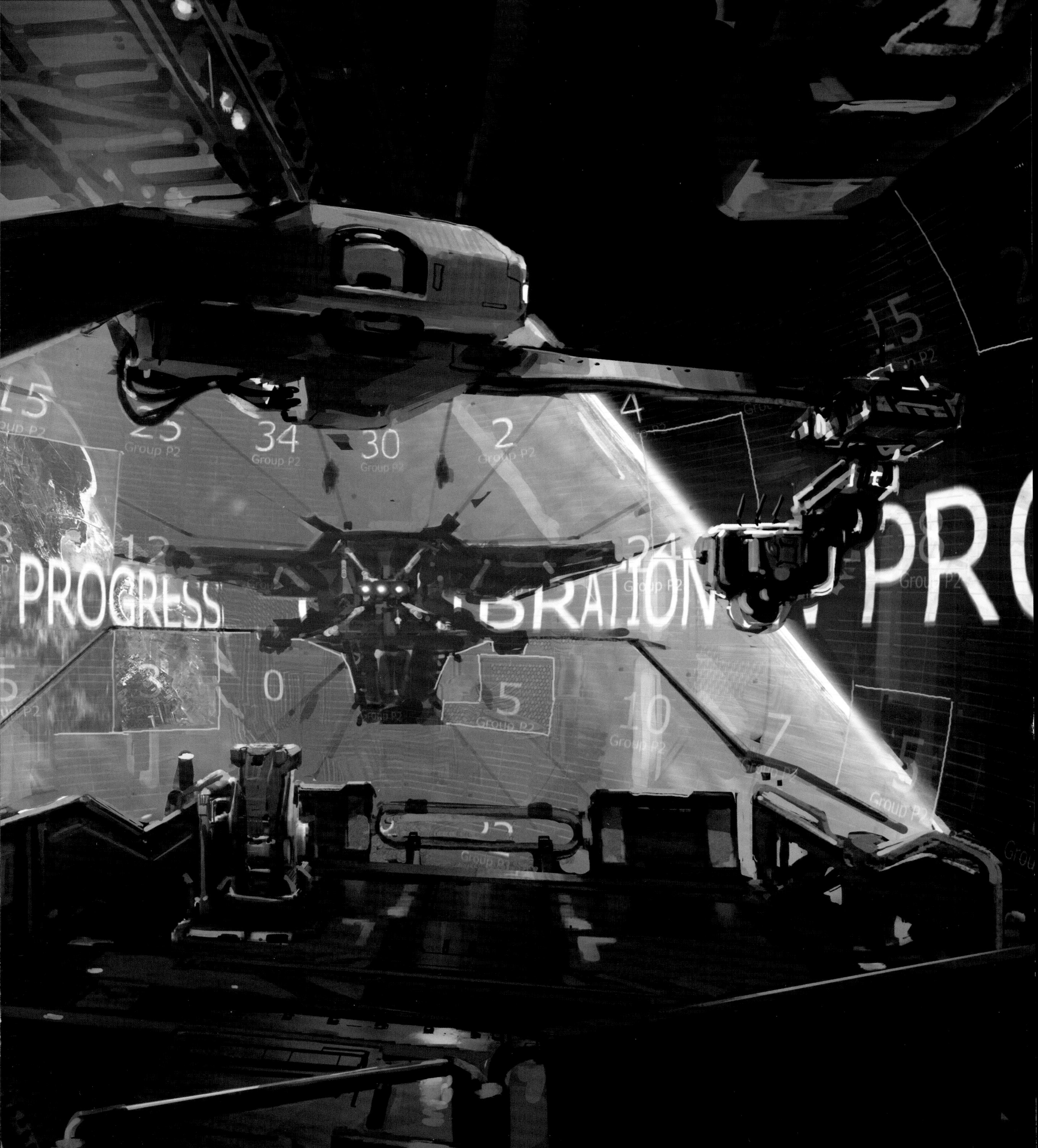

15
25
34
Group P2
30
Group P2
2
Group P2
4
PROGRESS
BRATION
PR
0
5
Group P2
10
Group P2
7

John Liberto

THE ART OF

HALO 5

GUARDIANS

INSIGHT EDITIONS

San Rafael, California

John Liberto

Shae Shatz

CONTENTS

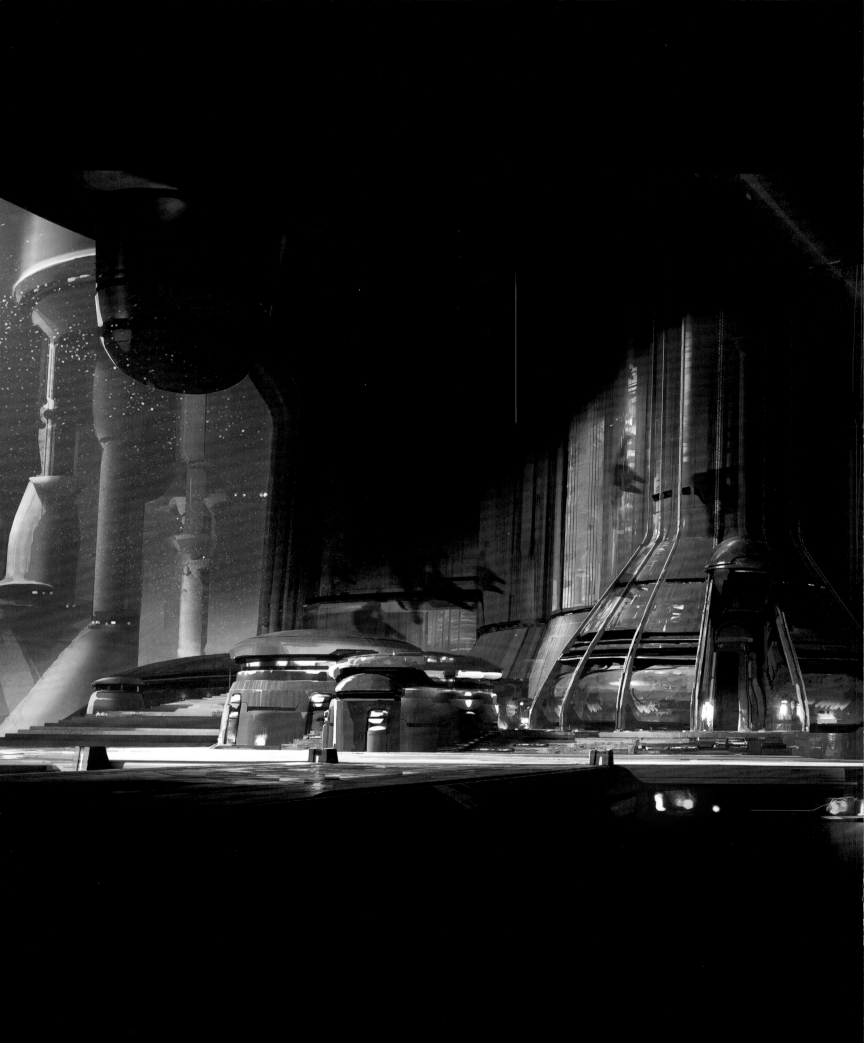

Darren Bacon

Kolby Jukes

FOREWORD
BY SPARTH

IT'S BEEN ANOTHER AMAZING THREE YEARS. Three years of intense creations to define *Halo 5: Guardians* and shape its multiple worlds. From the organic cities of Sanghelios to the rugged atmosphere of Meridian, we worked hard to imagine a new set of playing fields to discover and interact with. Bigger, stranger planets pushing even further the boundaries of architecture and geology.

Ahead of the production curve, you have concept artists. They're the guys who make the whole experience more concrete and reachable for production. They provide the feel of what's to come for an army of super creative minds eager to push the project forward. Simply put, they translate words into shapes and colors. But they obviously do much more, perfectly embedding themselves into the needs of all teams during all phases of production. This book goes way beyond concept art, though, as it includes works from many artists throughout 343 Industries who shaped environments, props, vehicles, and weapons with amazing scrutiny and dedication. This is their book.

I grew a lot from working on *Halo 5: Guardians*, but not in the way I would have expected. I thought I would have continued to be solely satisfied with my progression as an artist, the "Art Director's hat" being a cherry on top. But the opposite happened. I grew more interested in sharing. Sharing images, inspirations, techniques. Sharing victories and concerns. Sharing with artists who became friends. Again and again. It became a humbling experience where I would let go of my own art to better see and grasp the talent of others. But in this new balance, their successes were my successes, too, which was fantastically gratifying. I can't thank them enough for all these challenging and exhilarating moments.

If you jump into a concept artist's shoes, this is what you will see: the future. They literally conceive visions that are yet to come. They pave the way for games such as *Halo 5: Guardians* to fully materialize. It's no small task. It's daunting at times. But it's been an epic ride I would have missed for nothing in the universe.

343 Industries, assembling worlds one pixel at a time.

Sparth

Darren Bacon

INTRODUCTION
BY FRANK O'CONNOR

HALO IS AND ALWAYS HAS BEEN ABOUT its worlds and wonders. It's eponymous, in fact. Halo. For fans, the word itself conjures images of dizzying, vertiginous constructions and vast horizons that defy the imagination. Illustrations of places the player will pace and patrol. And the first step on our great journey is often art.

And that art comes in many forms. It can be literal napkin sketches—ideas or even fragments of ideas, rapidly captured to distill the essence of a thought or a place. It can be a detailed painting, a beautiful piece of concept art, the intent of which isn't simply to design a scene or an object, but to capture the very essence of how we wish the finished game to feel. As Nicolas Bouvier—better known as "Sparth"—took over the reins of Halo's art direction from the much-missed Kenneth Scott, it felt less like a jarring transition and more like a homecoming.

Sparth's art and imagination have for years inspired many of our other artists—artists whose work you'll see in these very pages—to make bigger, grander, more sweeping vistas; to create more scintillatingly realistic—or fantastic—spacecraft. To take seeds of ideas from the hearth of the imagination, and spark, then fan flames of intense creative reach.

The worlds of Halo are a contrast of styles—the grounded, oil-spattered metal and industry of human designs, the chitinous, iridescent majesty of Covenant forms, and the staggering, elegant brutality of massive Forerunner edifices. Three distinct visual languages. Three distinct species. Three distinct approaches to a universe filled with variety, humanity, and alien wonder. And as we think about variety, we should think about the analog this has within the team. The different talents that make up the images and ideas you see in the game.

We have painters. We have sculptors. We have people profoundly prosaic in pen and ink. We have 3-D modelers; we have color specialists; we have artists and animators whose role is to make fire dance, explosions emote, and smokes and mists and vapors bilious, brilliant, and believable. Halo games have never been about photo-realism—although there are elements of that captured in its fidelity. Rather it has always been about a painterly style. A rich and ravishing blend of hues and silhouettes that speaks directly to the player's imagination and builds experiences bigger than reality and more magical than simulation. Halo is an artist's game.

Our painters, our sculptors, our colorists, and our effects experts are given constant encouragement and latitude to stretch their talents and strain their ability—to unleash the dreams they had when they first picked up a paintbrush or a piece of clay. And these art books are a catharsis of sorts—to take the joy and wonder of the process and the prototyping phase, and share it with readers and connoisseurs who revel in its completion as much as we do during its creation. So here's to the artists, here's to the universe, and here's to you, the player who gets it, and gets how hard and worthwhile it is.

Sparth

John Liberto

01 PRE-PRODUCTION

John Liberto

BEFORE WORLDS ARE BUILT, THEY MUST BE IMAGINED

We started the first concepts for *Halo 5: Guardians* in 2012. From the very beginning of the project, our goal was to push and expand on the Halo saga in big, bold ways visually. We wanted to press at the seams of our new worlds via imaginative, rich environments that would give players opportunities to explore the edges of the ever-expanding Halo universe. As shepherds of the franchise, our goal was to deliver on our expectations, knowing that the only limit to our creativity was our own imaginations, and that is a pretty humbling place to start as artists. —Sparth

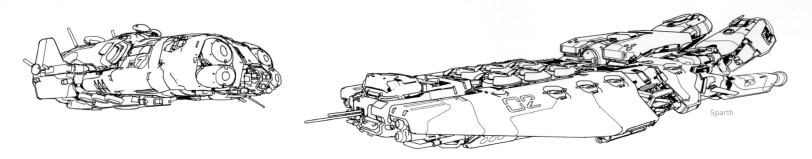

Sparth

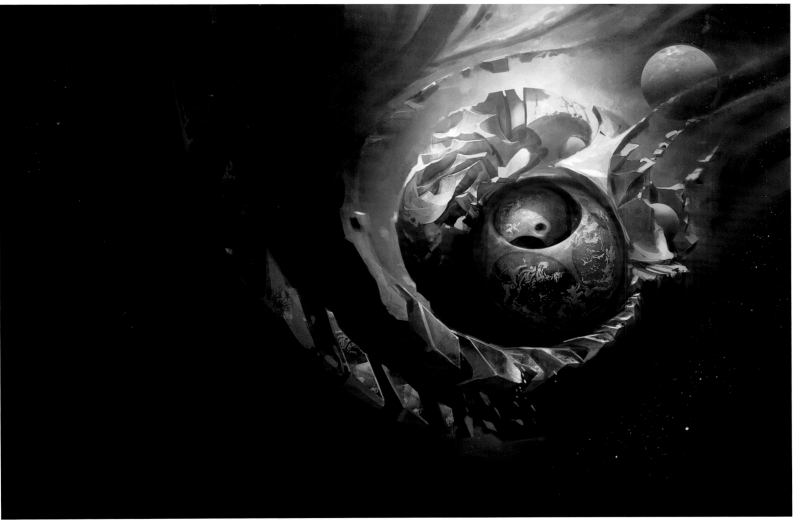

John Liberto

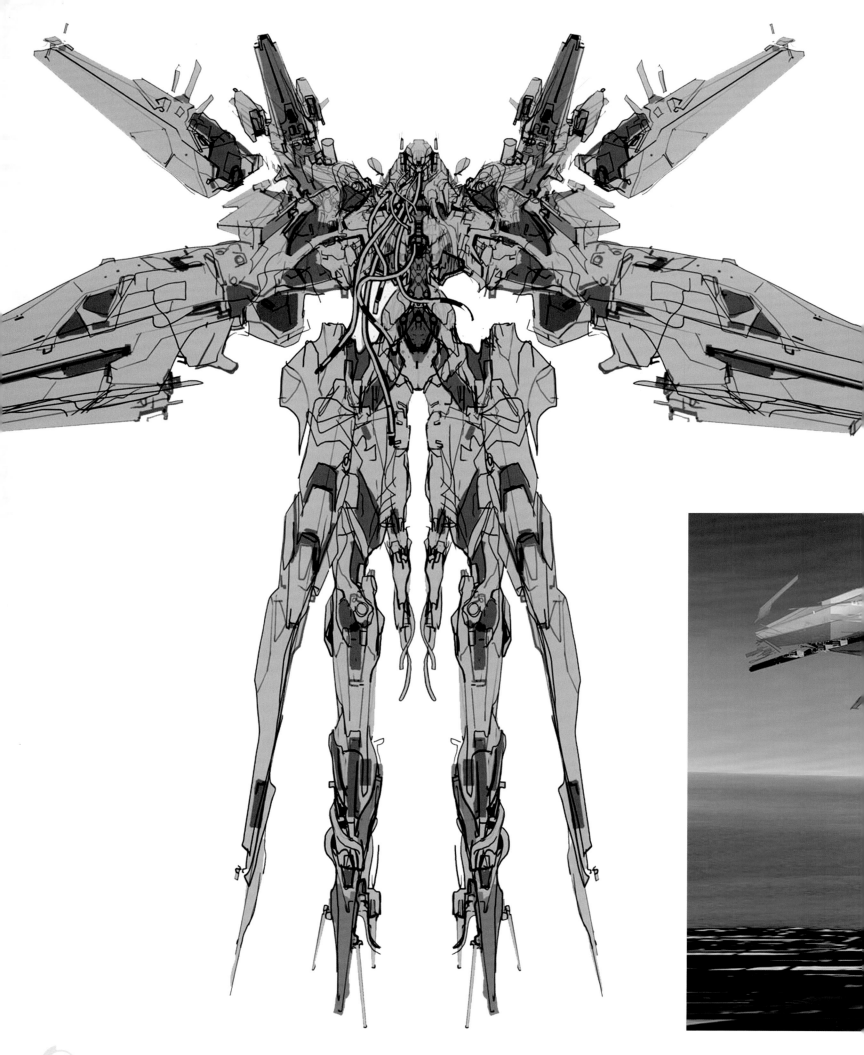

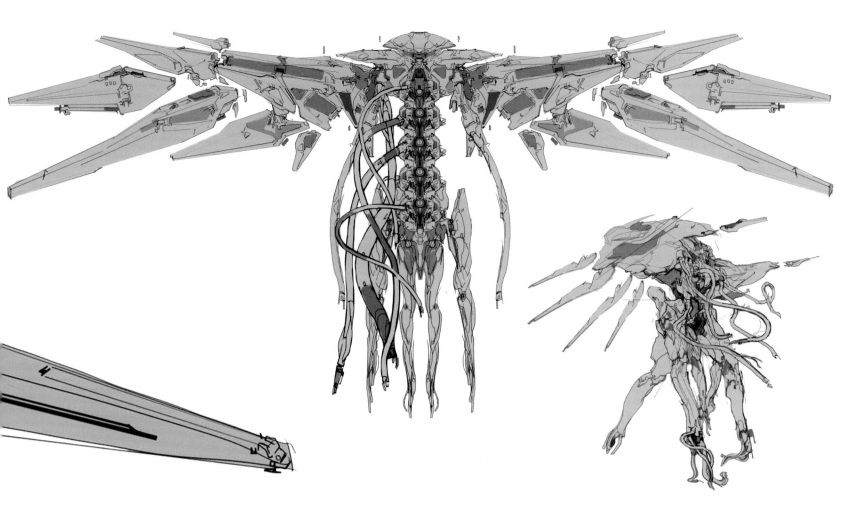

THESE PAGES: Robogabo

"At this stage in production, we in concept start with a very loose idea that has trickled down from the writers or studio creative director and begin chipping away at the problem as if trying to reveal a sculpture from marble." —*Sparth*

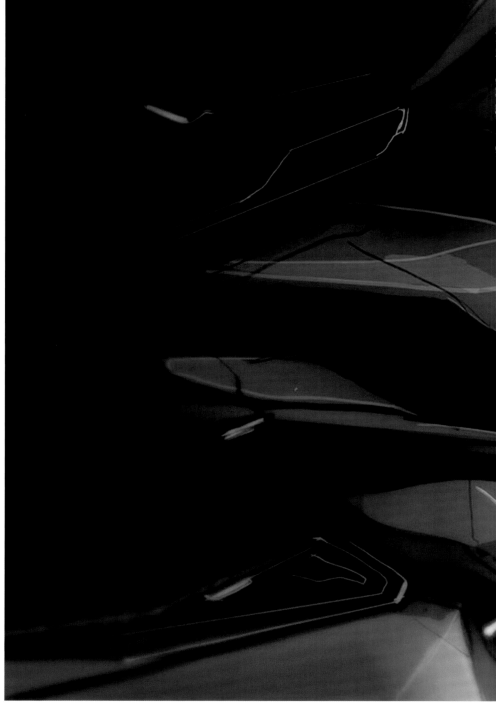

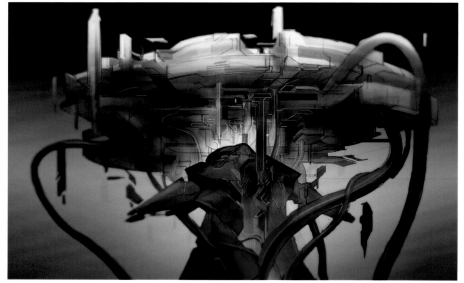

THESE PAGES: Robogabo

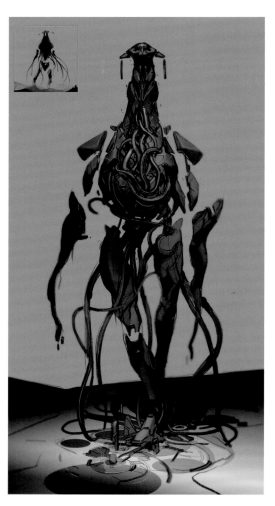

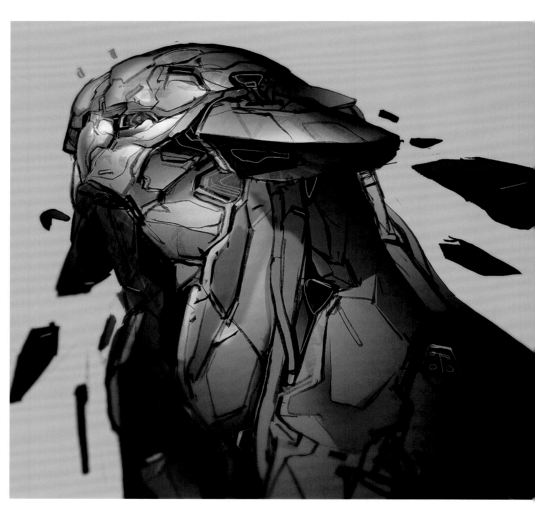

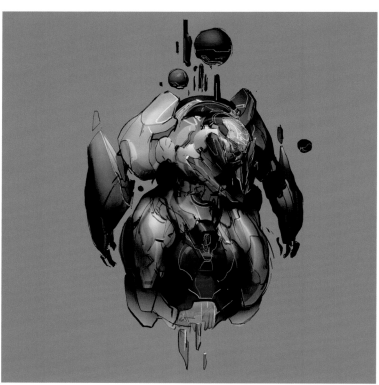

THESE PAGES: Robogabo

"When we only know Chief as his armor, it's difficult to find ways to convey subtle emotions. The cloak worked nicely as a metaphor, showing that Chief was hurting from Cortana's loss, and he was hiding himself from that hurt until he could hide no more." —*Brian Reed*

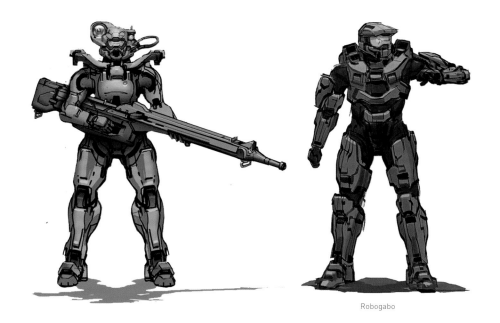

Robogabo

John Liberto

THIS PAGE: Robogabo

THESE PAGES: John Liberto

John Liberto

Sparth

02 ENVIRONMENTS

Darren Bacon

BUILDING A GALAXY

Halo is known for its big reveals and sense of epic-ness. As an environment artist, you want to help create those reveal moments and deliver on the epic, expansive feel of the universe. Through that you hope to invite a process of discovery—the way you discover a new space, the way you go through it, the way that space is known to you, the way it's alien to you. It's part of not only the visual experience, but also the gameplay experience. In *Halo 5: Guardians*, it's a process of discovering the galaxy. —Sparth

Sparth

Shae Shatz

Darren Bacon

—◢KAMCHATKA

An unsettled world, too harsh for most life, Kamchatka appears to have been a Forerunner communication network hub. Of little interest to any but the most intrepid adventurers, Kamchatka remains unexplored.

Axis; Concept art by Gareth Hector

THESE PAGES: Sparth

UNSC FLEETS

Both the UNSC *Infinity* and *Argent Moon* have their roles in the fleet. *Infinity* is the flagship and at 3.5 miles long is home to thousands of the UNSC's best and brightest, who place their lives on the line daily. As for *Argent Moon*, her purpose was always something darker . . .

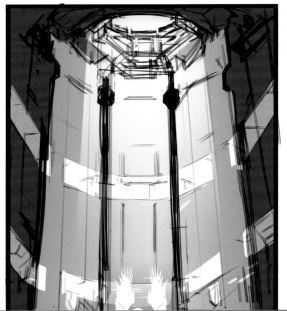

"The overall art direction of the *Infinity* falls in line with contemporary UNSC design languages. The artistic objective of the massive ship is to offer the viewer a narrative 'home base' for the level of advancement the human race has achieved while simultaneously showcasing sophisticated sci-fi visuals that we as artists (and fans) yearn to see and share with the world." —*Darren Bacon*

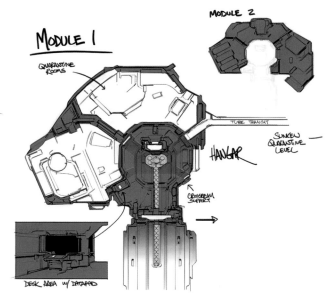

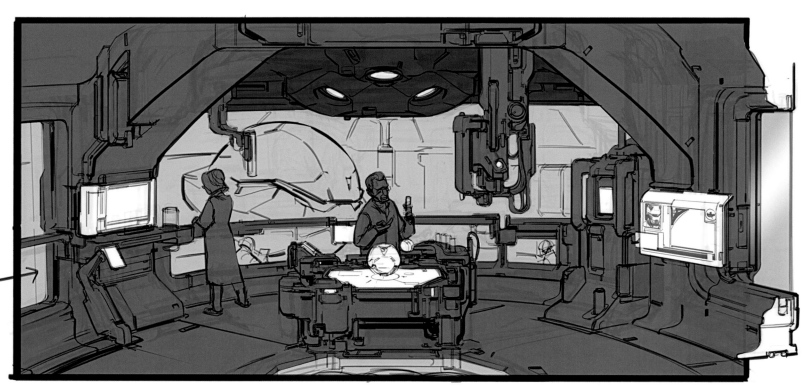

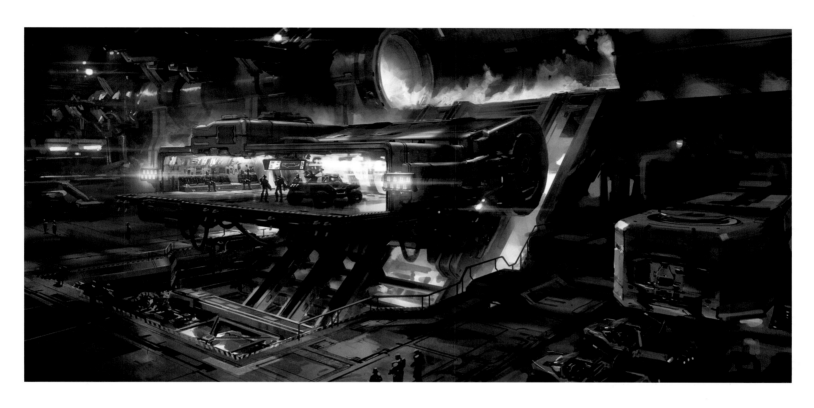

THIS PAGE: John Liberto

Sparth and David Bolton

UNSC DATAPAD

PERSONAL "KEY"?

A

B

C

D

ABOVE AND RIGHT: Justin Oaksford

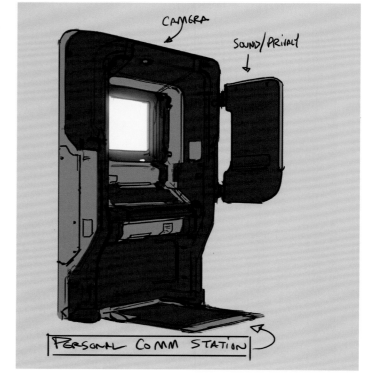

CAMERA

SOUND/PRIVACY

PERSONAL COMM STATION

ABOVE AND BELOW: Shae Shatz

Sparth

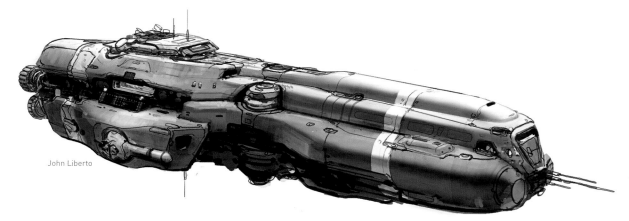

John Liberto

John Liberto

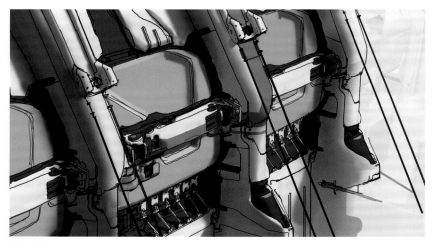

Daniel Chavez

Sparth

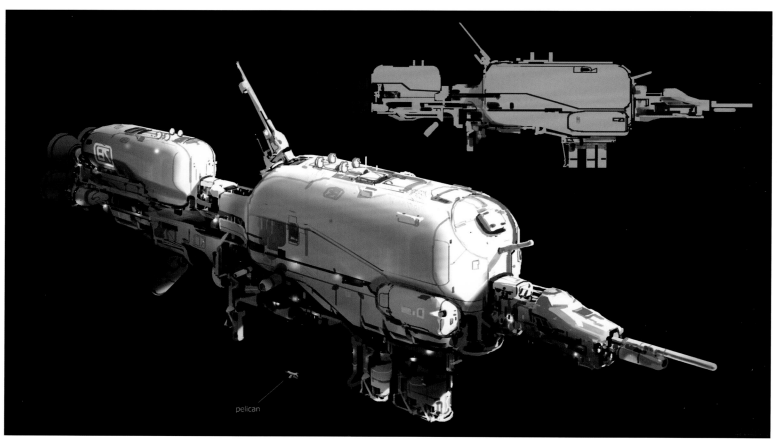

pelican

Sparth

Sparth

Kory Lynn Hubbell

MERIDIAN

A former colony world, glassed by Covenant forces during the Human-Covenant War, Meridian now lies beyond UNSC jurisdiction, controlled by the Liang-Dortmund Corporation.

Sparth

"The Meridian style in general is similar to UNSC but even more industrial. In this environment, things don't need to be decorative or polished, just functional." —*Justin Oaksford*

Paul Richards

John Liberto

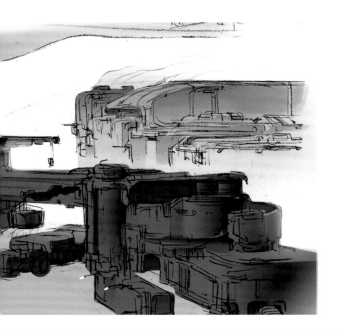

John Liberto

"On Meridian you have pockets of miners and engineers who have been reterra-forming and making areas livable. Everything on Meridian comes from off-world, so you have spaceships coming in and dropping necessities for infrastructure, but it all has a temporary and prefabricated look." —*Sparth*

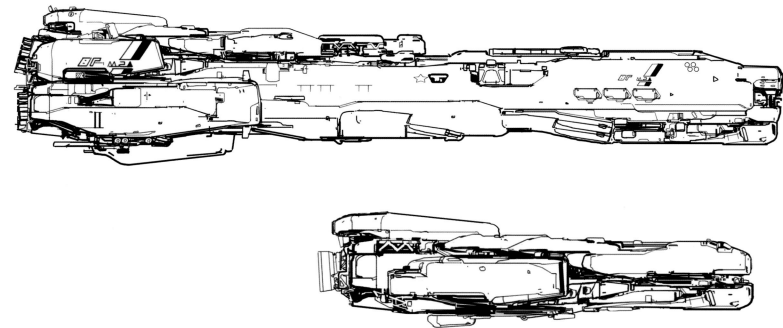

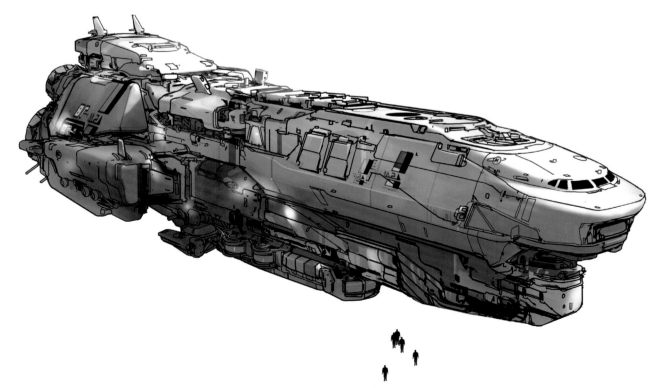

65

Sparth

John Liberto

"With Meridian we were trying to make it feel human without crossing over into UNSC territory but also make it look like they had repurposed some military equipment." —*Kory Lynn Hubbell*

"If there's no plausible story behind something, it shouldn't be there. For example, in the image below, we originally wanted a fountain. Through multiple discussions, we decided that maybe a fountain isn't the best fit for a mining town. So we have a tree instead. We felt that there is no better symbol for nature than a tree. You have this very bleak landscape with all these industrial buildings around, but then there's this fake tree in the middle of it. It's almost comedic, but it's also logical—if you're forced to live in a barren landscape but have the technology to simulate nature, it's logical to do so." —*Kory Lynn Hubbell*

Kory Lynn Hubbell

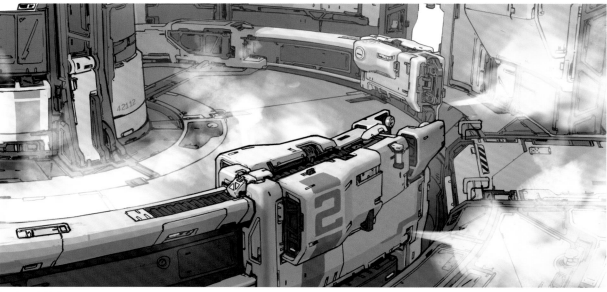

Kory Lynn Hubbell

John Liberto

David Bolton

John Liberto

John Liberto

"This is the first time that we go to the Elite home world, so we wanted to explore some of their indigenous culture—what their culture would have been like before the Covenant came to extend their influence over it. So we had a lot of influences emerging from ancient, unconventional, martial cultures in human history." —*Glenn Israel*

SANGHELIOS

The Elite home world, Sanghelios is a landscape almost unknown to human eyes. As the Arbiter fights to unite his people, this is the world where the Covenant make their last stand.

Sparth

John Liberto

Shae Shatz

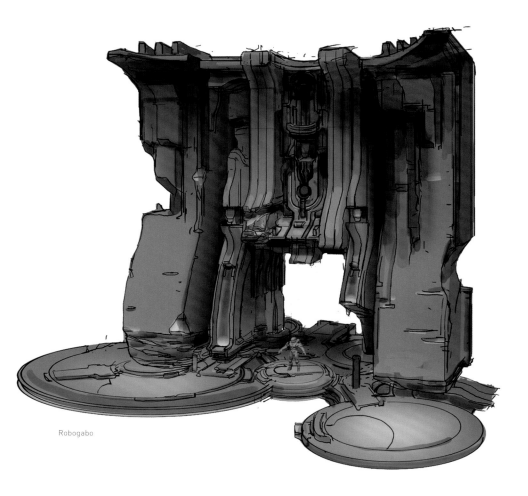
Robogabo

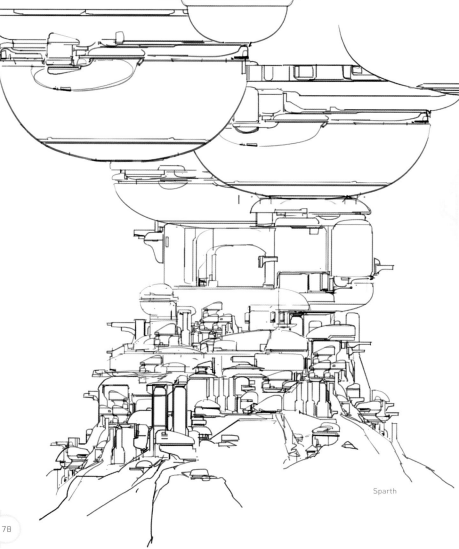
Sparth

"In designing an environment, you take what you know about the civilization and work outward from there. Glenn Israel, who has done a lot of work on Sanghelios, starts with really specific things when he begins designing a new world. For example, he'll ask himself what the hands of the indigenous species look like. Then he builds out from there. Once you know what the hand looks like, then you know what their writing might look like and that informs the architecture, which informs everything else." —Darren Bacon

Darren Bacon

Justin Oaksford

Sparth

"When it came time to start working with hieroglyphics, we were looking at Islamic, Mongolian, and Indian art as well as other cultures that adopted a more pictographic or logogrammatic approach to language, such as Egyptian and Mayan hieroglyphics. The architecture came first, and the language was built around that to express things that we wanted to say about the Elite culture and the things that they found aesthetically pleasing, such as curved shapes and circular motifs." —Glenn Israel

Janet Ung

Glenn Israel

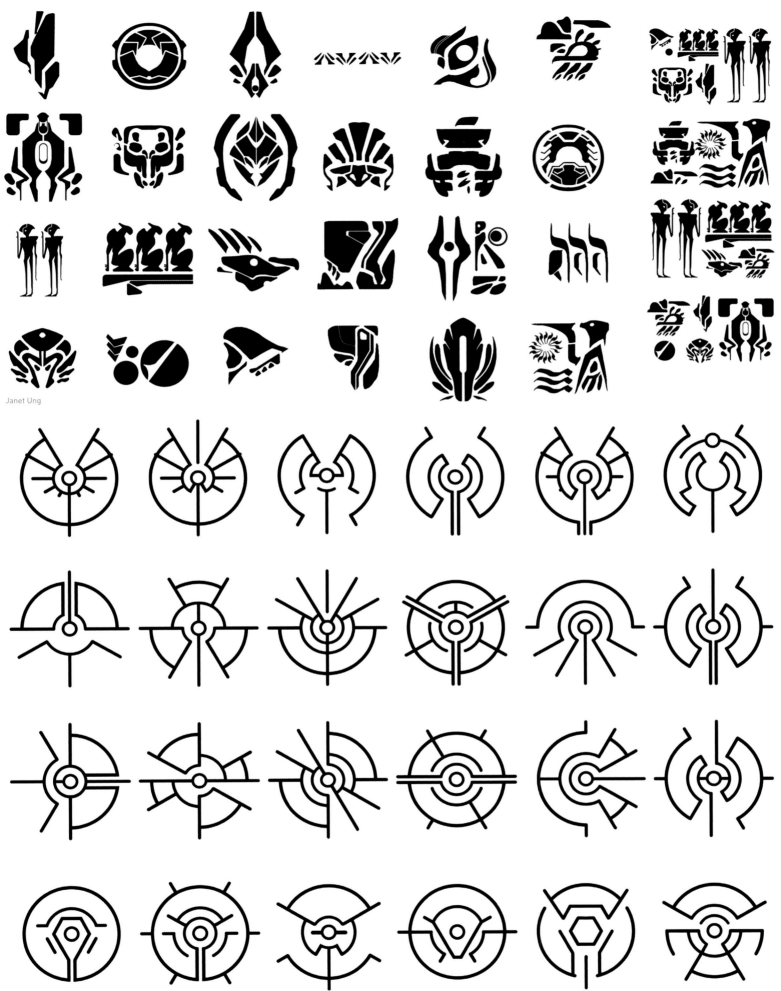

Janet Ung

Glenn Israel

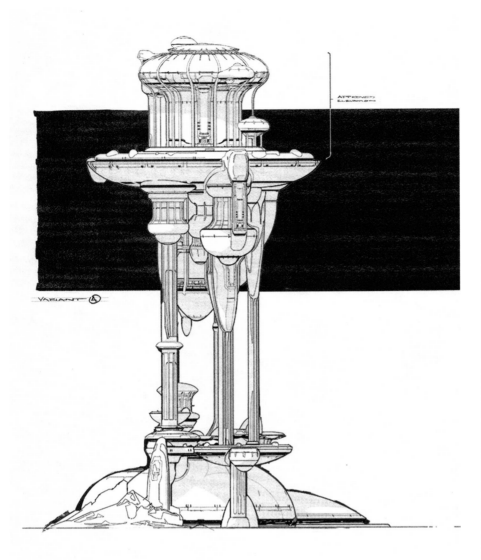

ABOVE: Darren Bacon
BELOW: Sparth

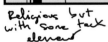

Religious but with some tech element

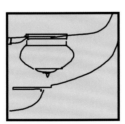

Revised DOME

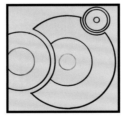

PACMAN "eating circles" derived from water Ripples

"The Sangheili architecture clearly has an alien feel. It's the Elite home world, meaning that a specific faction of the Covenant has been living here. These people are very bulky, very warrior-like, very alien, too. When it comes to Sanghelios, parts of it are warm, desertlike. You have a lot of canyons and, as a result, a lot of the architecture has been built into the sides of these canyons." —Sparth

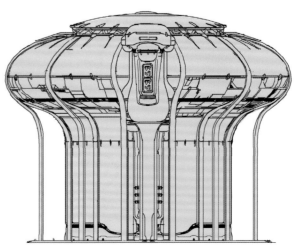

ABOVE AND OPPOSITE BOTTOM: Sparth

John Liberto

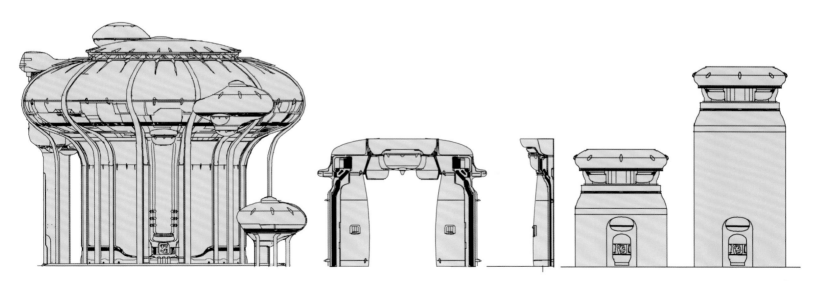

Darren Bacon

GENESIS

Genesis is a Forerunner Builder facility constructed to act as a connection between the digital world of the Forerunner Domain and our physical realm.

Sparth

John Liberto

John Liberto

"For Genesis we developed this concept of a fractal-based world with fractal plant life, such as terrestrial corals. We used this concept to create an alien world that hasn't really been seen before in science fiction. There are still familiar elements, but it's a very unique environment. It also contrasts well with the desert environments you experience on Sanghelios. So you have this contrast between a desert with an ancient civilization and a completely alien, fractal world with lots of color." —Darren Bacon

John Liberto

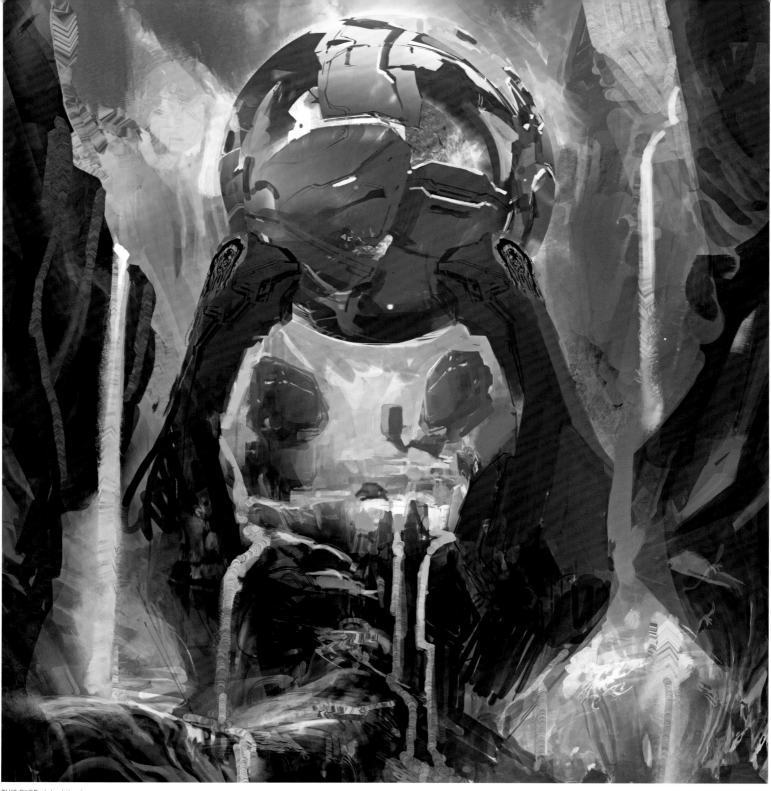

THIS PAGE: John Liberto

ABOVE: John Liberto BELOW: Kory Lynn Hubbell

Darren Bacon

ABOVE AND OPPOSITE TOP: Paul Richards **BELOW:** Darren Bacon

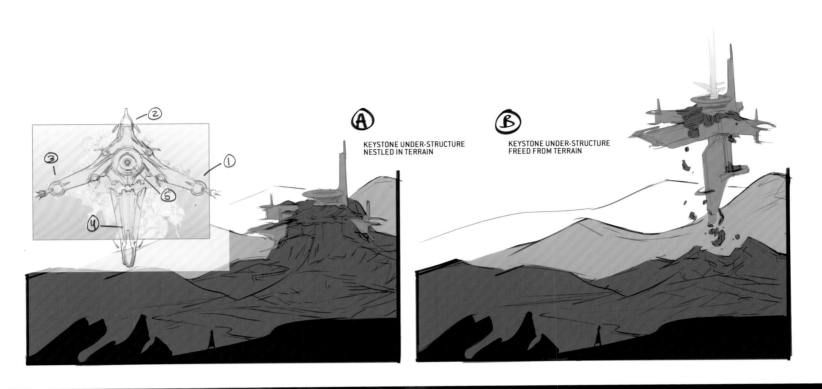

Ⓐ KEYSTONE UNDER-STRUCTURE
NESTLED IN TERRAIN

Ⓑ KEYSTONE UNDER-STRUCTURE
FREED FROM TERRAIN

THIS PAGE: John Liberto

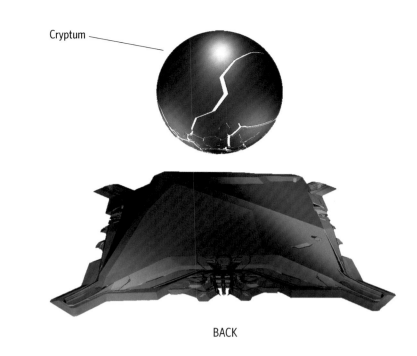

Cryptum

BACK

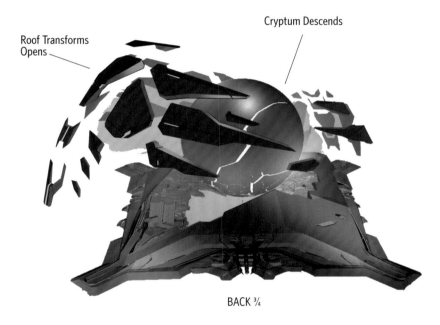

Roof Transforms
Opens

Cryptum Descends

BACK ¾

Cryptum Fully
Descended

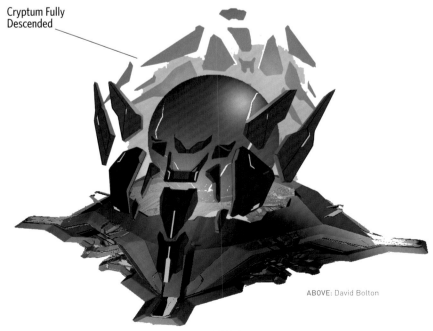

ABOVE: David Bolton

FRONT

"The Forerunner grew Genesis—it's a totally
artificial planet—so the landscape reflects the
aesthetic of their technology in many ways."

—Kory Lynn Hubbell

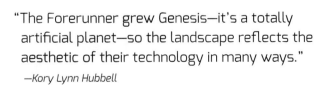

THIS PAGE: Darren Bacon

ABOVE AND BELOW: Sam Brown and Jihoon Kim

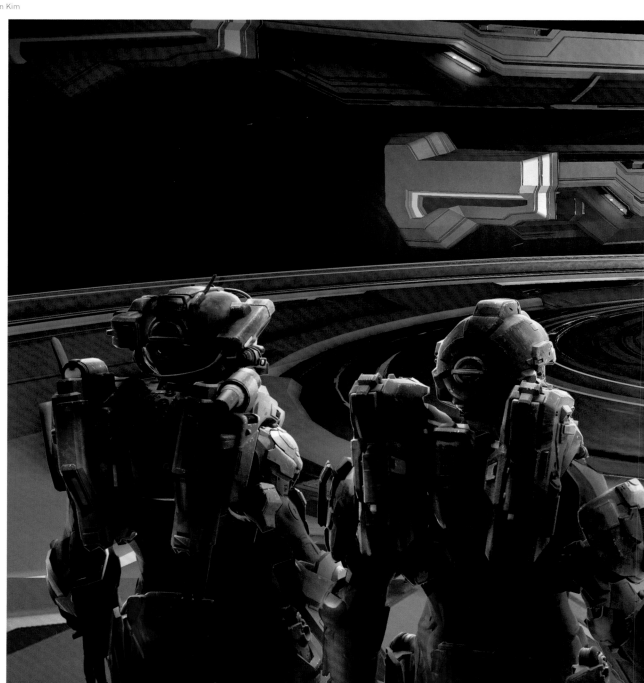

Sparth

Kory Lynn Hubbell

John Liberto

CHARACTER DESIGN

When you put eight specific characters into a game and you're creating eight different armors with eight different personalities, it's a huge creative task, but it will be exciting to play. There's a lot of variety when you play these characters, because they all have different visuals and different features when it comes to their armors and weapons. They also have their weapons of choice with different skins connected to them. That's a lot of context, and it was a challenge. —Sparth

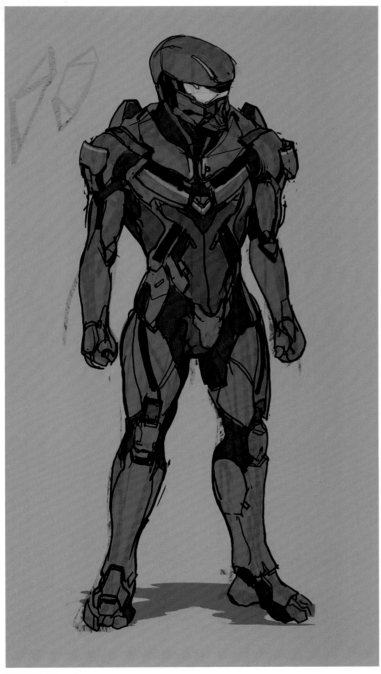

THIS PAGE: Robogabo

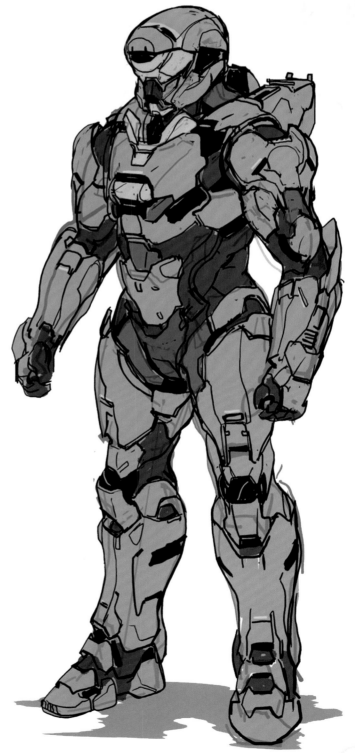

Daniel Chavez

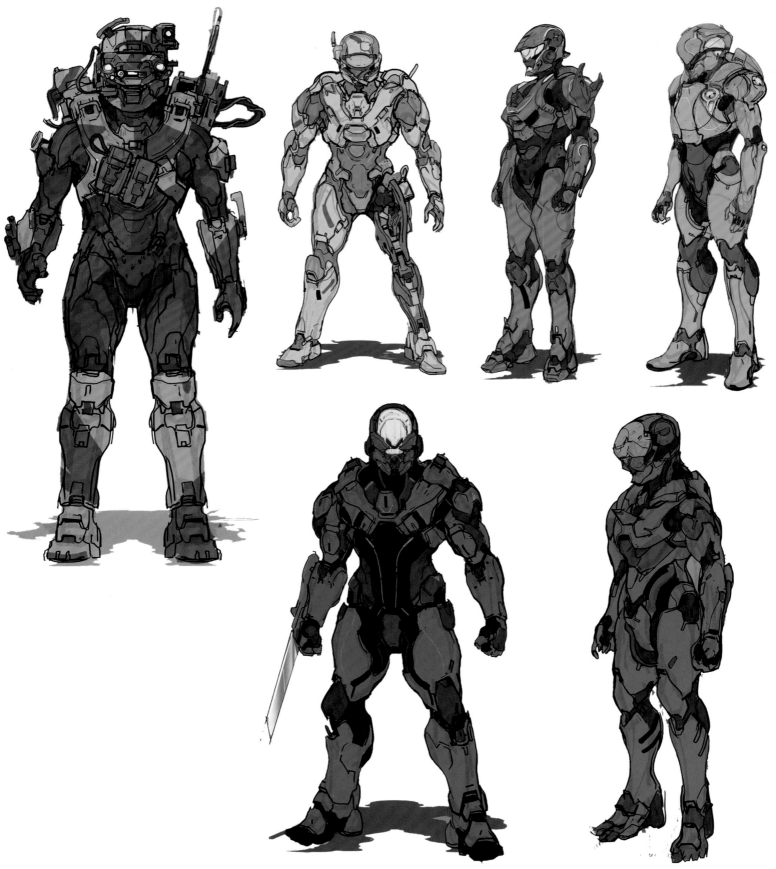

⎯⎯/UNSC

The United Nations Space Command (UNSC) is humanity's vanguard among the stars. As Sparth explains, "from an aesthetic standpoint, we don't normally see the Spartan's faces. Most of the time, we're going to see them with their helmets on, in badass mode. This is what we focus on. We want them to be badass. That's the important thing."

Kory Lynn Hubbell

"Blue Team uses an older generation of armor—
it's a bit clunky and closer to today's way of
building tanks. Fireteam Osiris's armor is a lot
more futuristic, featuring curvy lines and cables
that are thoughtfully placed. It's optimized and
researched." —*Daniel Chavez*

TOP AND ABOVE: Robogabo

Alex Cunningham

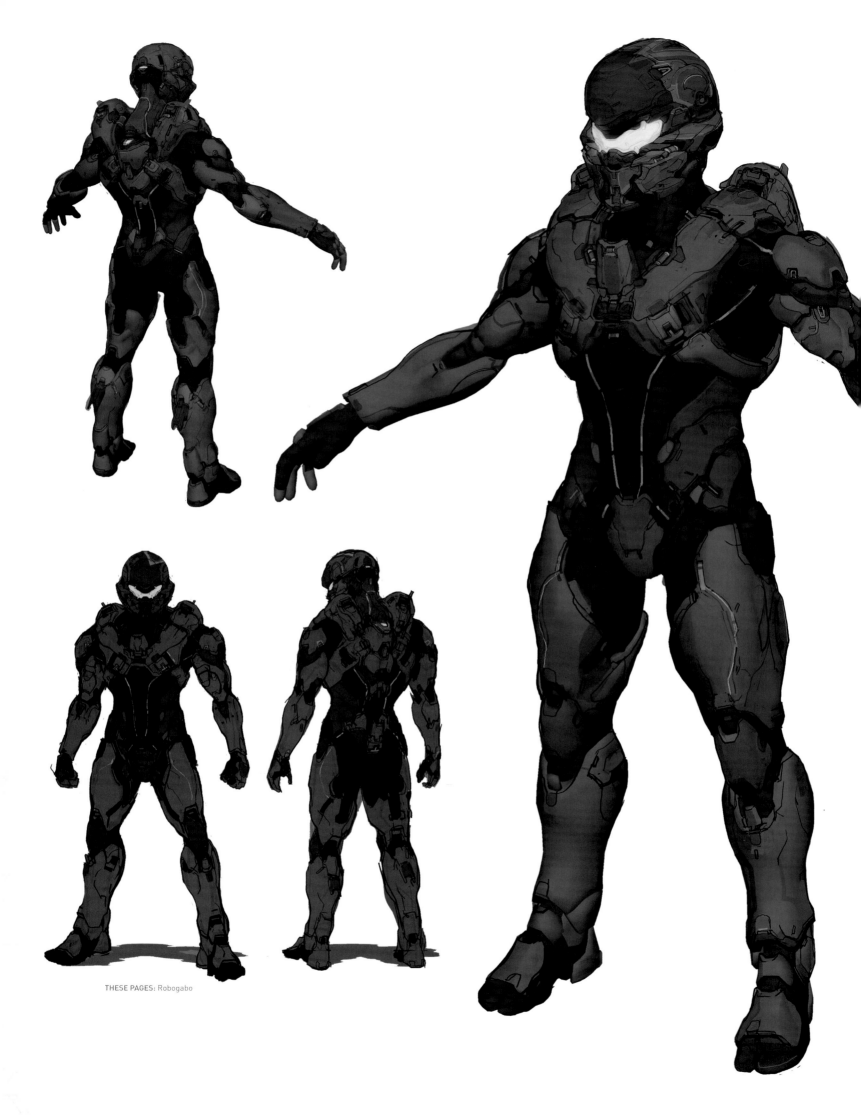

THESE PAGES: Robogabo

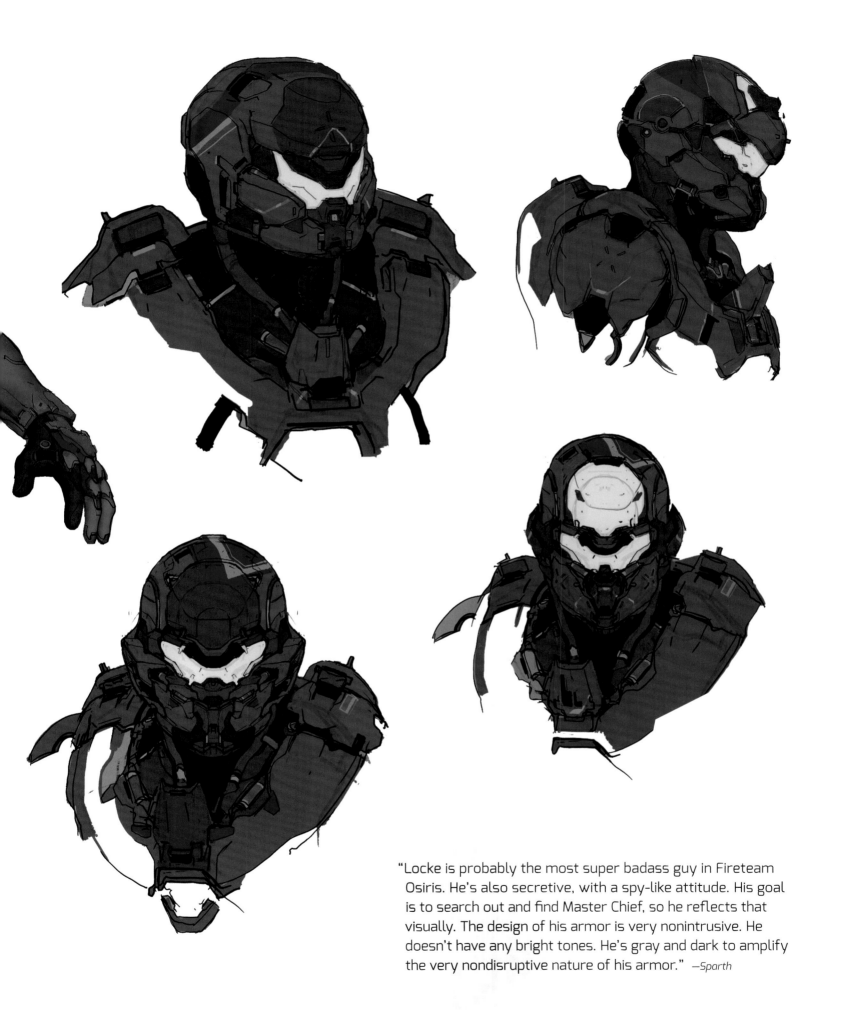

"Locke is probably the most super badass guy in Fireteam Osiris. He's also secretive, with a spy-like attitude. His goal is to search out and find Master Chief, so he reflects that visually. The design of his armor is very nonintrusive. He doesn't have any bright tones. He's gray and dark to amplify the very nondisruptive nature of his armor." —*Sparth*

"Physically, Vale is very sturdy, but she's also extremely agile. This is reflected not only in her armor but also in her form, which is quite slick. The magenta color of her armor is also significant, as it implies nervousness and aggression." —*Sparth*

THESE PAGES: Robogabo

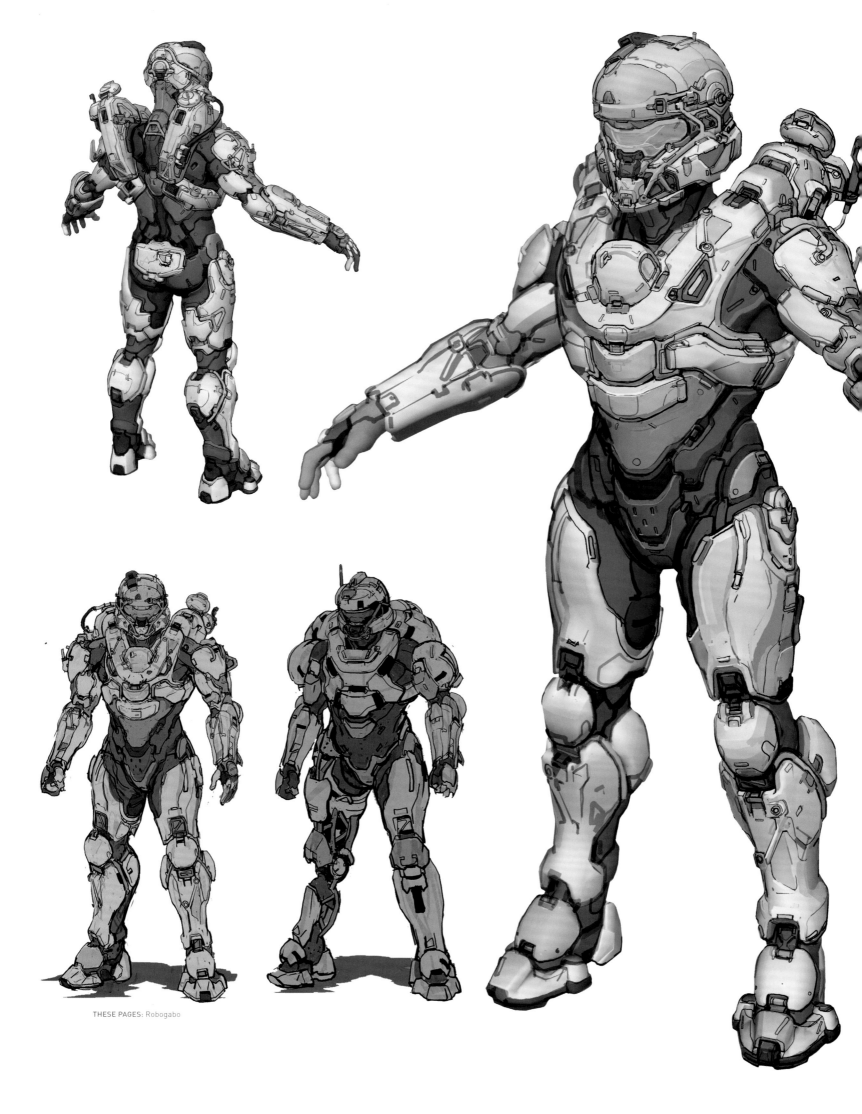

THESE PAGES: Robogabo

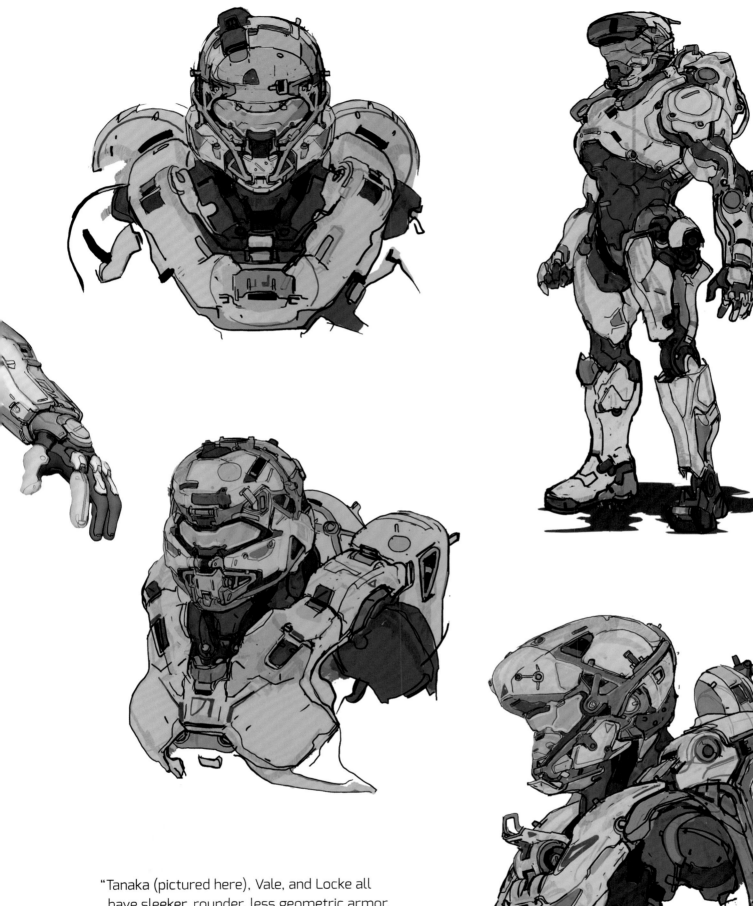

"Tanaka (pictured here), Vale, and Locke all have sleeker, rounder, less geometric armor, which makes it feel like their armor is more custom-built for them and not mass-produced and then fitted onto their body." —*Justin Oaksford*

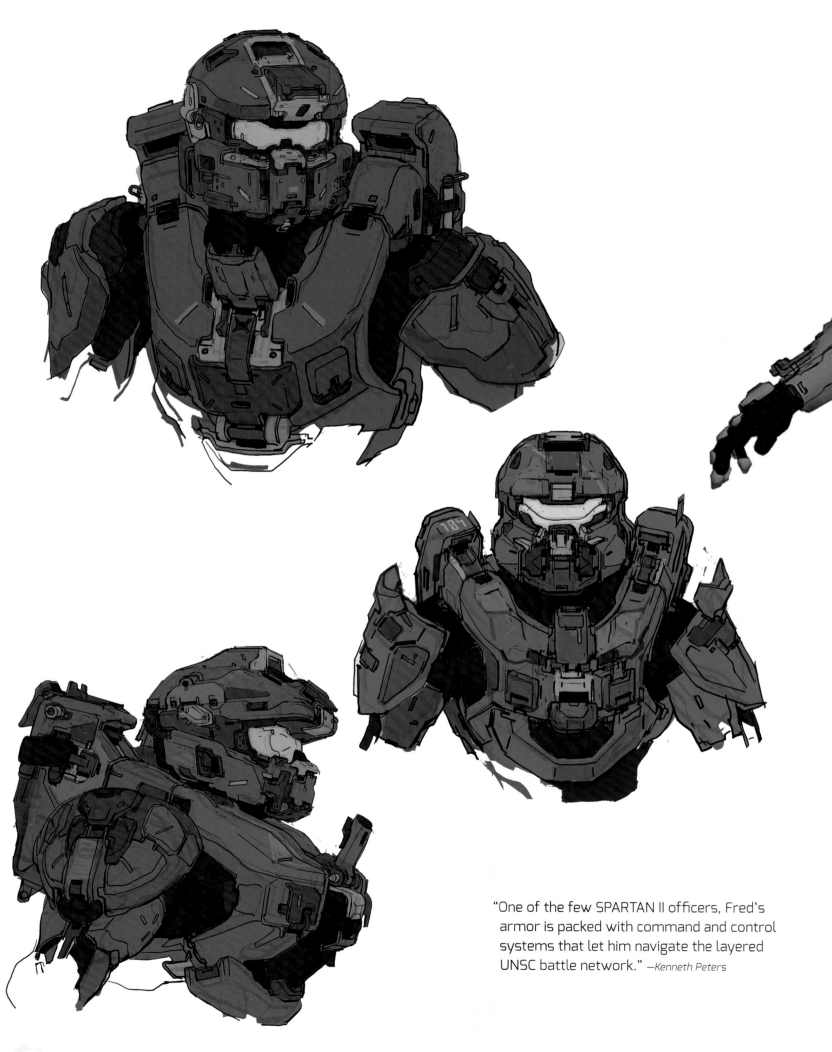

"One of the few SPARTAN II officers, Fred's armor is packed with command and control systems that let him navigate the layered UNSC battle network." —*Kenneth Peters*

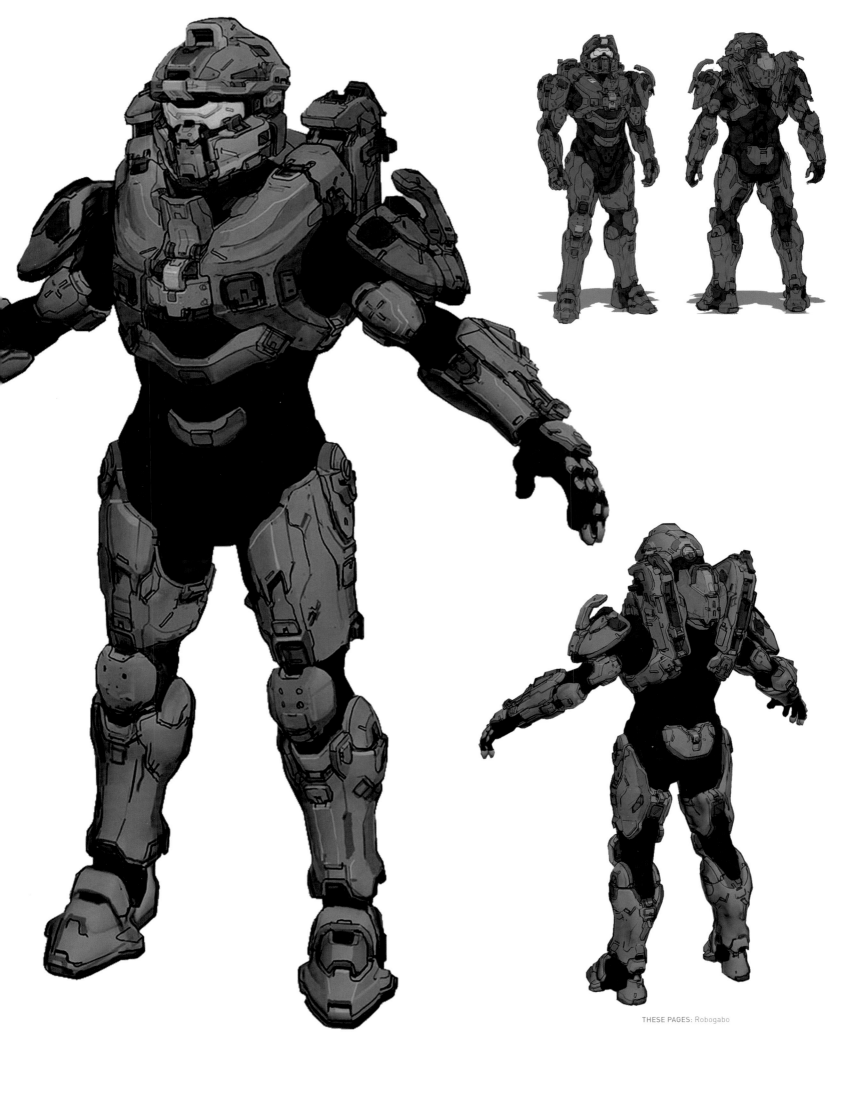

THESE PAGES: Robogabo

THESE PAGES: Robogabo

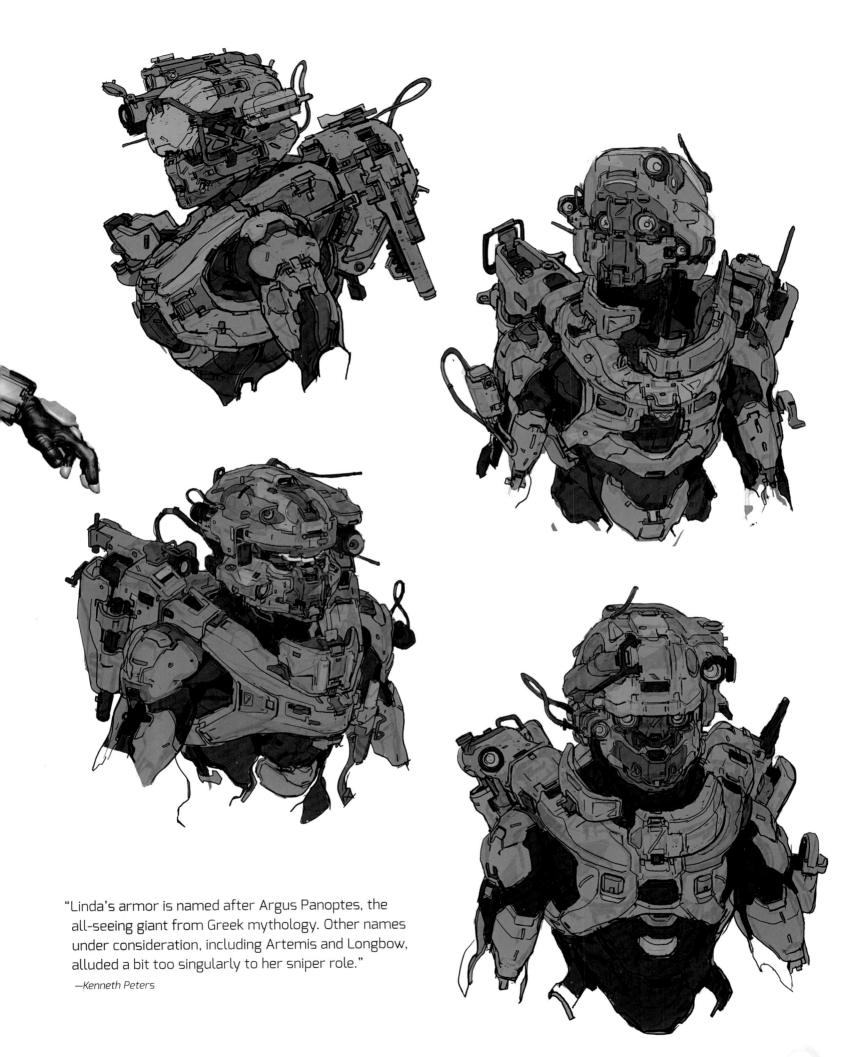

"Linda's armor is named after Argus Panoptes, the all-seeing giant from Greek mythology. Other names under consideration, including Artemis and Longbow, alluded a bit too singularly to her sniper role."

—Kenneth Peters

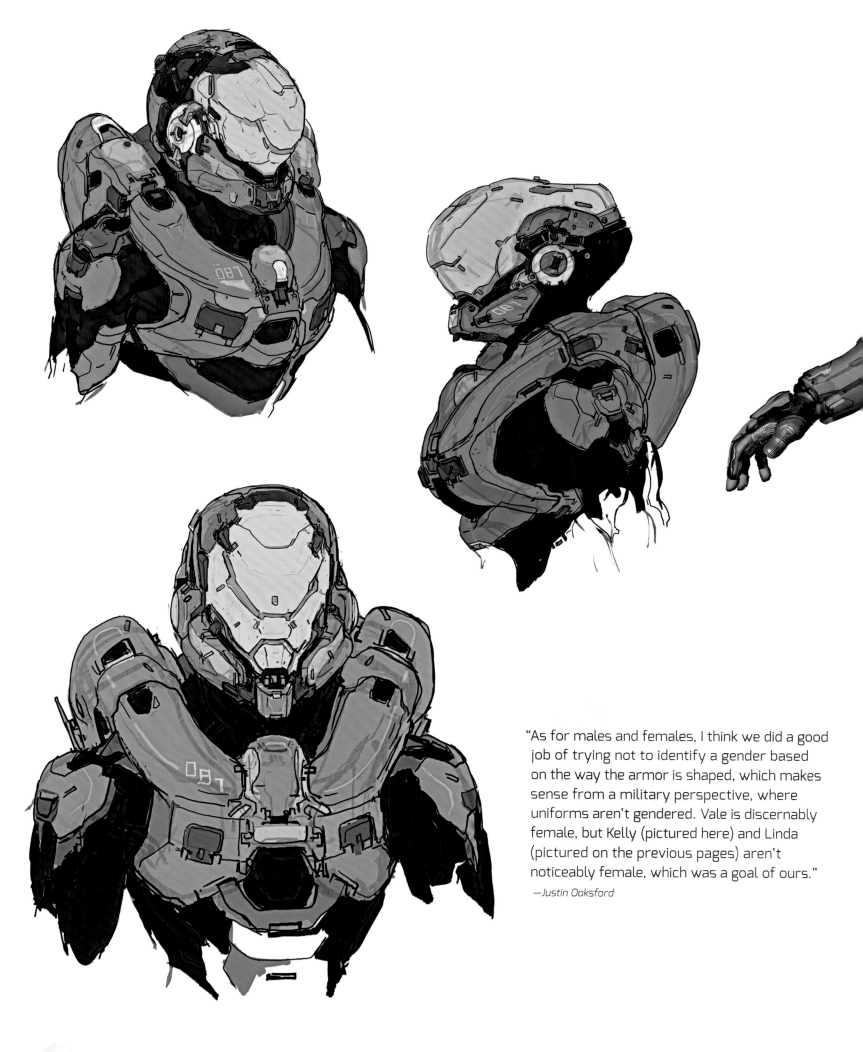

"As for males and females, I think we did a good job of trying not to identify a gender based on the way the armor is shaped, which makes sense from a military perspective, where uniforms aren't gendered. Vale is discernably female, but Kelly (pictured here) and Linda (pictured on the previous pages) aren't noticeably female, which was a goal of ours."

—Justin Oaksford

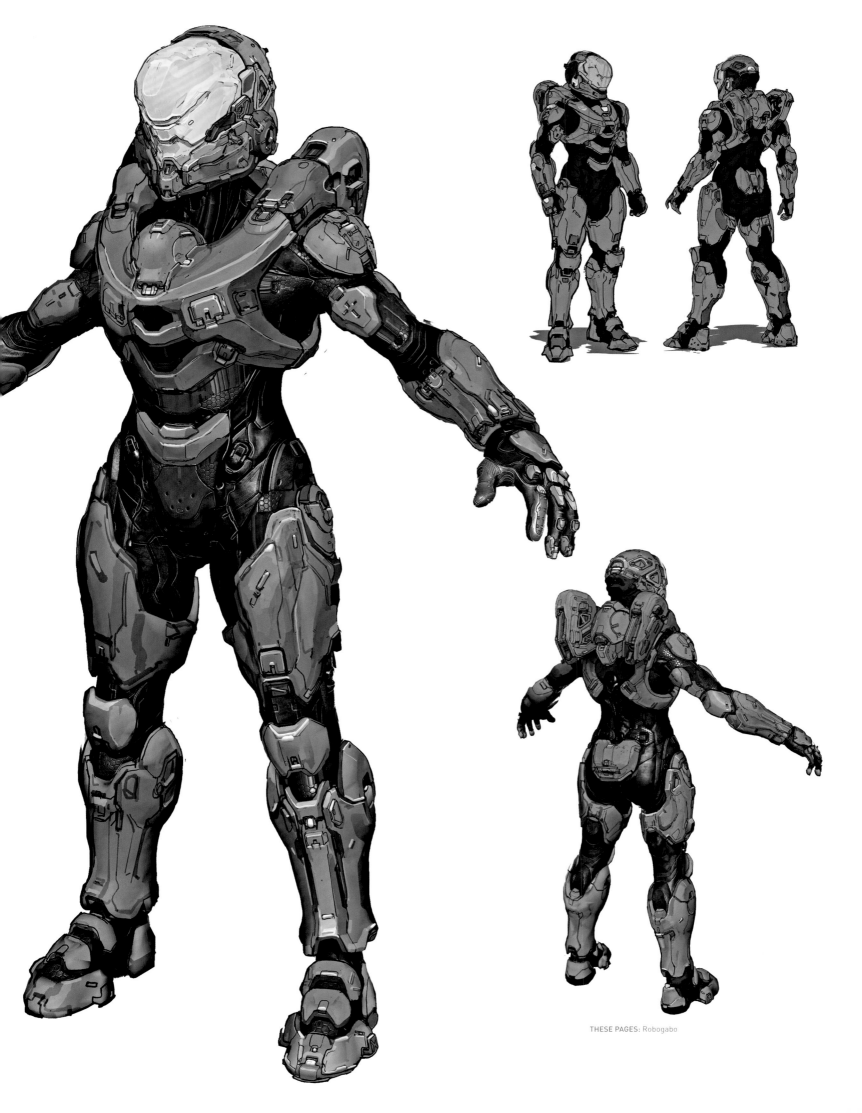

THESE PAGES: Robogabo

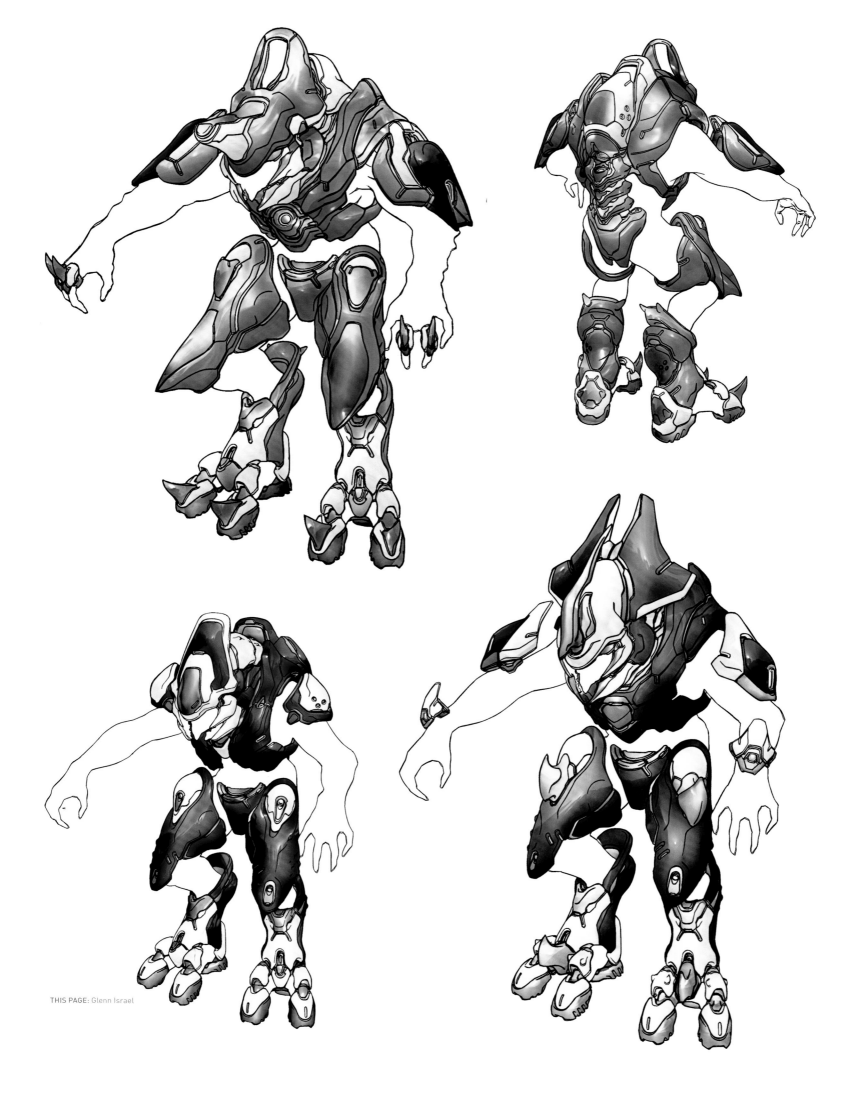

SWORDS OF SANGHELIOS

The Arbiter's forces have taken the name Swords of Sanghelios in their war to extinguish the Covenant's false light and bring about a lasting peace. As Sparth articulates, "the Swords of Sanghelios are involved in a revolution on their planet. They are disconnected from the Covenant-loyal Elites because religiously they are very different. As a result, this is the first time that we really differentiate them from the Covenant."

THIS PAGE: John Liberto

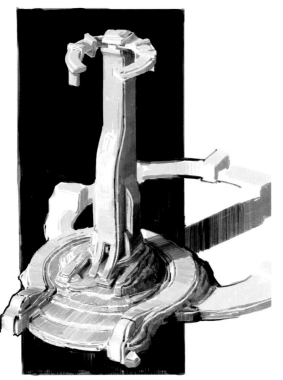
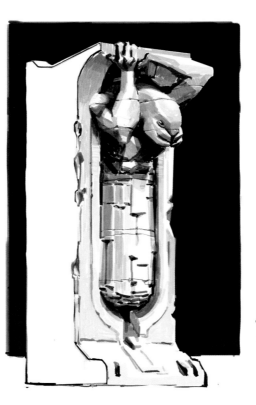
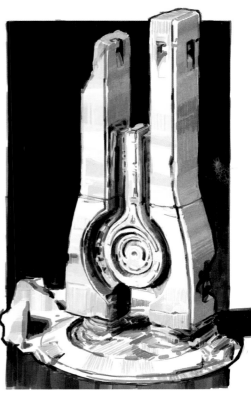

Glenn Israel

Kolby Jukes

Glenn Israel

Glenn Israel

"The Arbiter is an interesting character because his armor is very antiquated; it's very medieval compared to everything else in the game. It's made of all-natural materials like bronze, and the body suit is made of leather." —*Kolby Jukes*

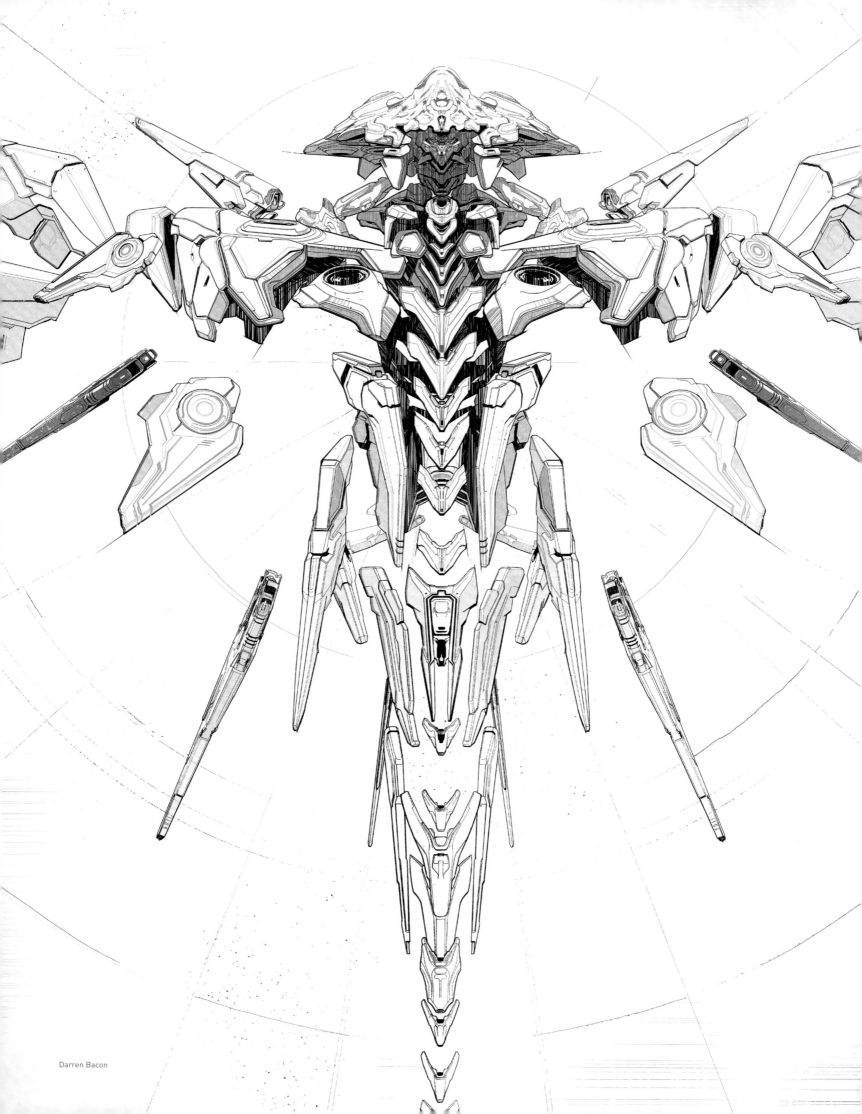

Darren Bacon

FORERUNNER

The Forerunners are gone, but many of their advanced automated forces remain. The Composed essences of the Promethean Knights, and the ancilla-driven Soldiers, Crawlers, and Watchers form the ranks of an undying and infinitely replenishable army of artificial warriors.

BACKPACK BITS
SEPARATE

THIS PAGE: Paul Richards

Kolby Jukes

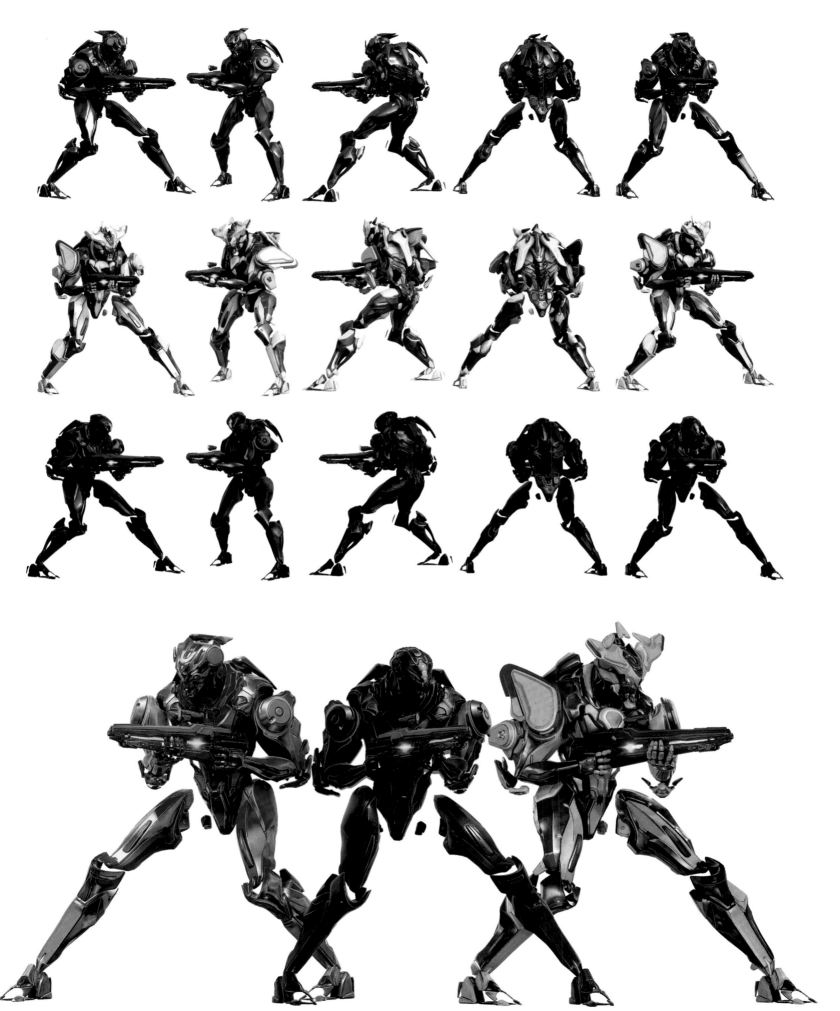

THESE PAGES: Kolby Jukes

135

Paul Richards

Stephen Dyck and Jaemus Wurzbach

Stephen Dyck

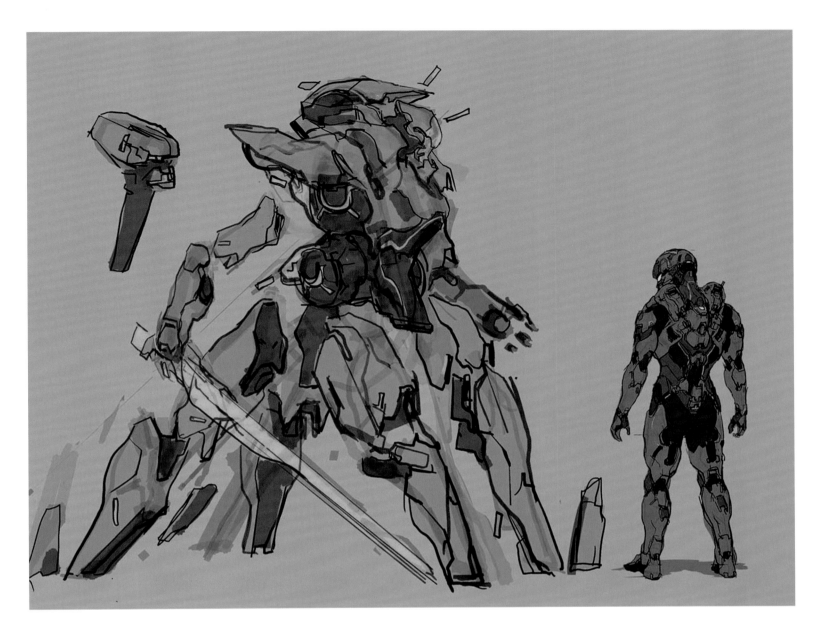

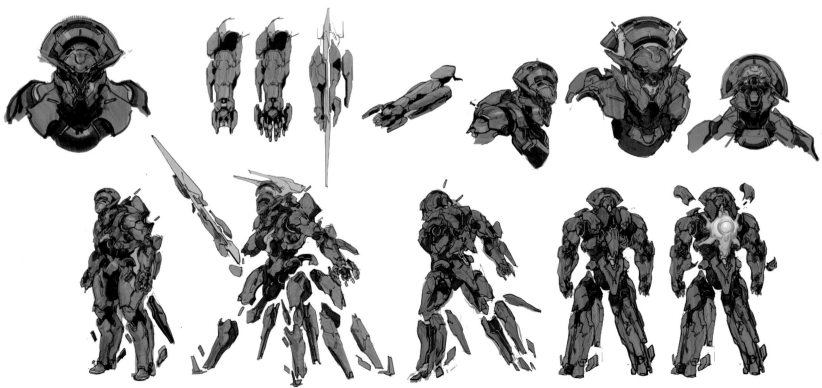

THIS PAGE: Robogabo

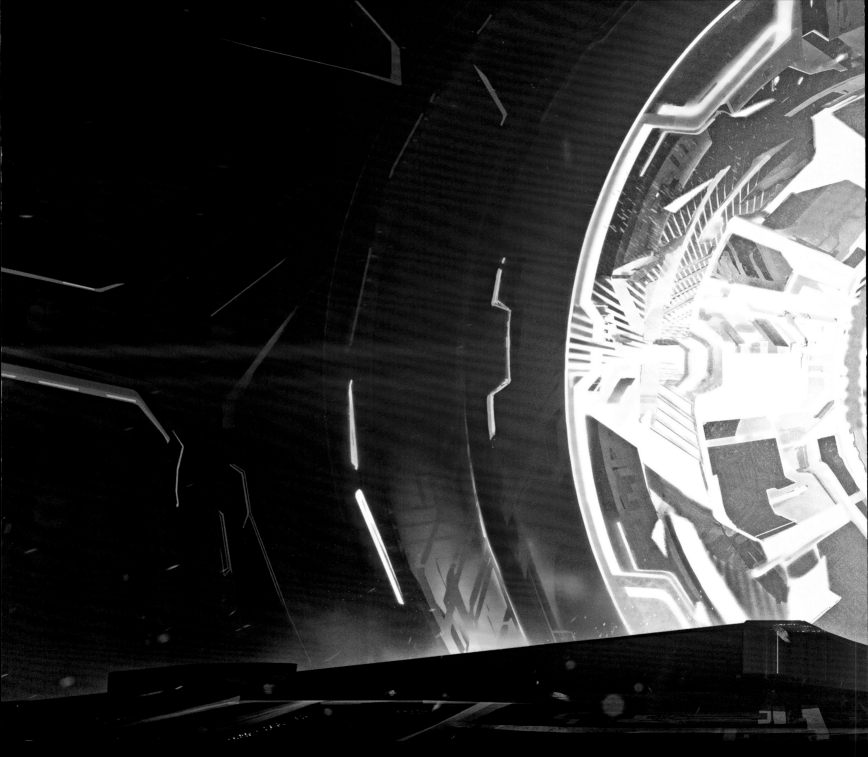

Kory Lynn Hubbell

"Throughout Halo, scale is very important. Verticality is a key word that we use very often when we want to create a scenario where the player is forced to look up. The Forerunner Guardian is part of that. The Guardian is very imposing—something you want to reach but is so much bigger than you are." —*Sparth*

Kolby Jukes and Sean Binder

Kory Lynn Hubbell

Kolby Jukes

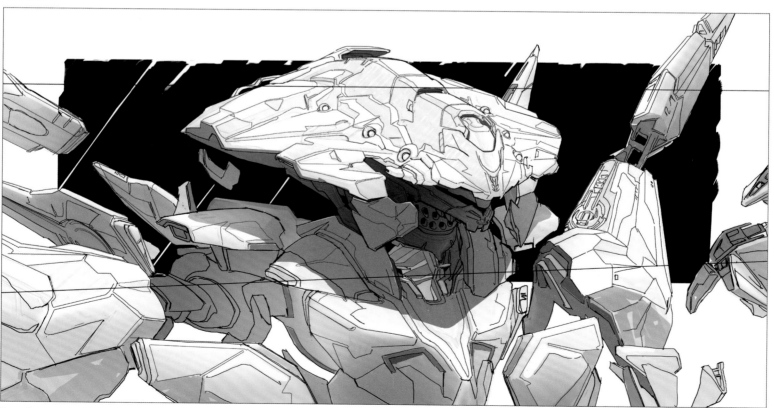

Darren Bacon

"The Guardian is a brand new thing. There were many early versions—bipeds with tentacles, bird-like iterations. Building something like this for the game is very, very challenging. The Guardian is massive, and we have to detail it and give it a complexity to match its size." —*Kolby Jukes*

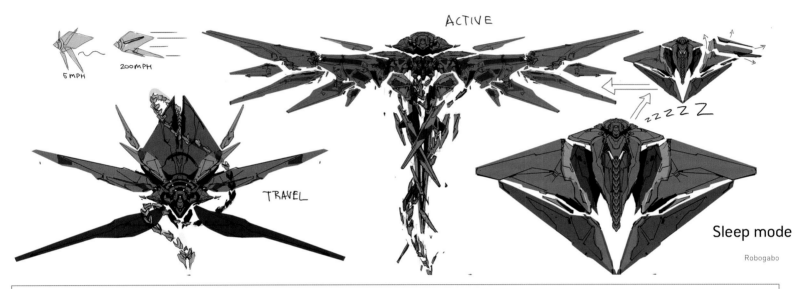

ACTIVE

5 MPH

200 MPH

TRAVEL

zzzzz

Sleep mode

Robogabo

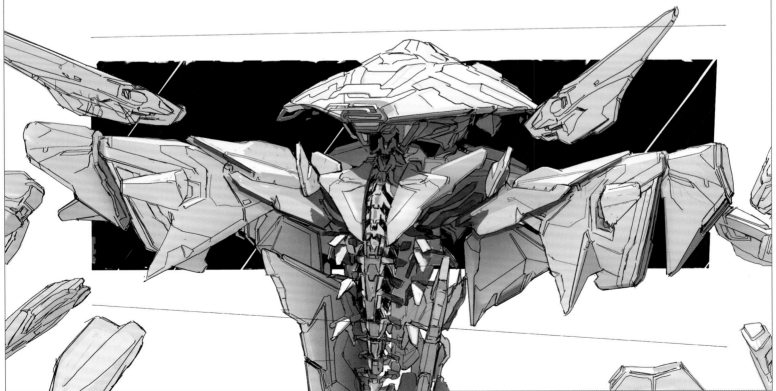

Darren Bacon

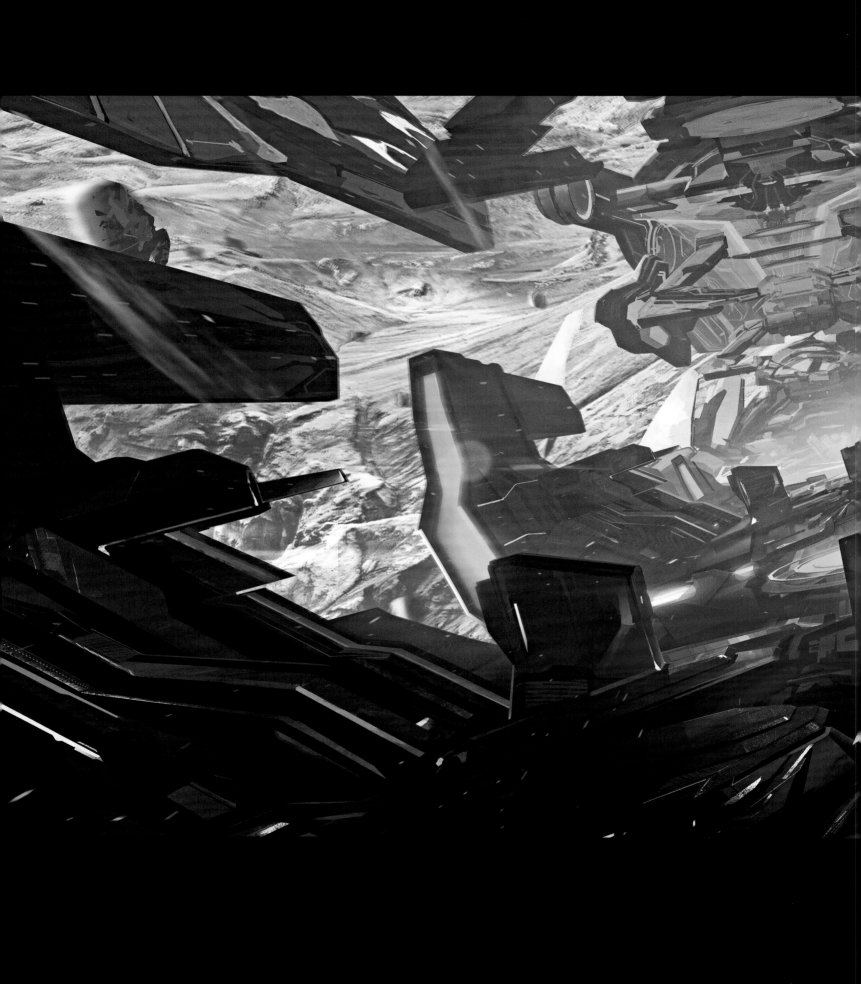

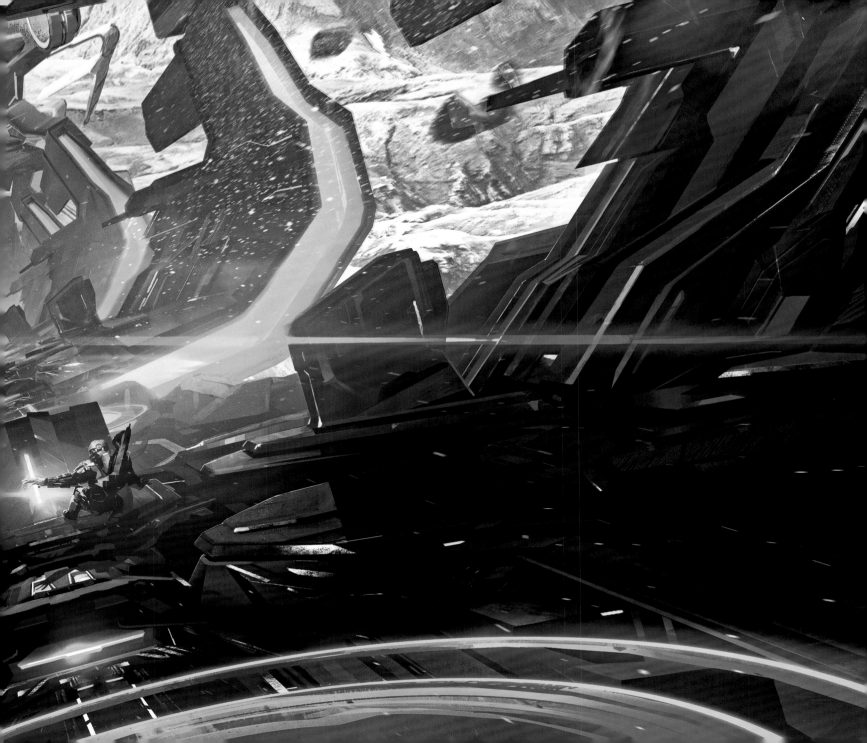

John Liberto

04 | WEAPONS

Sparth

WEAPON DESIGN

When it comes to weapon design, I'm obsessed with function. Any time we think about additions or new features for the weapons, we always have function in mind. I am always asking myself why we are going to add a specific type of feature to a weapon—whether it is changing the size of the barrel or putting a scope on top of the gun. Why are we doing it, and what type of impact on function is it going to have? Function drives our weapon design. As a result, it gives a more concrete sense of reality. If you add something only for the pure, abstract sake of it, it's never going to make sense. You need the design to make sense functionally, especially when it comes to weapons. —Sparth

Kenneth Scott

Andrew Bradbury

John Liberto

UNSC WEAPONS

The galaxy is a dangerous place. You'll need a weapon.

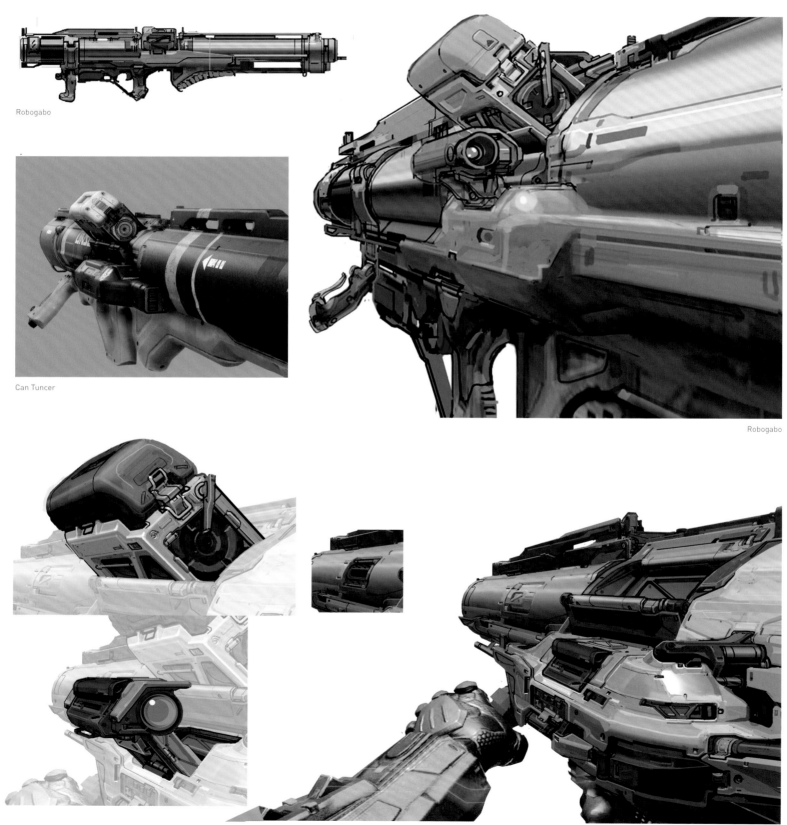

Robogabo

Can Tuncer

Robogabo

Robogabo

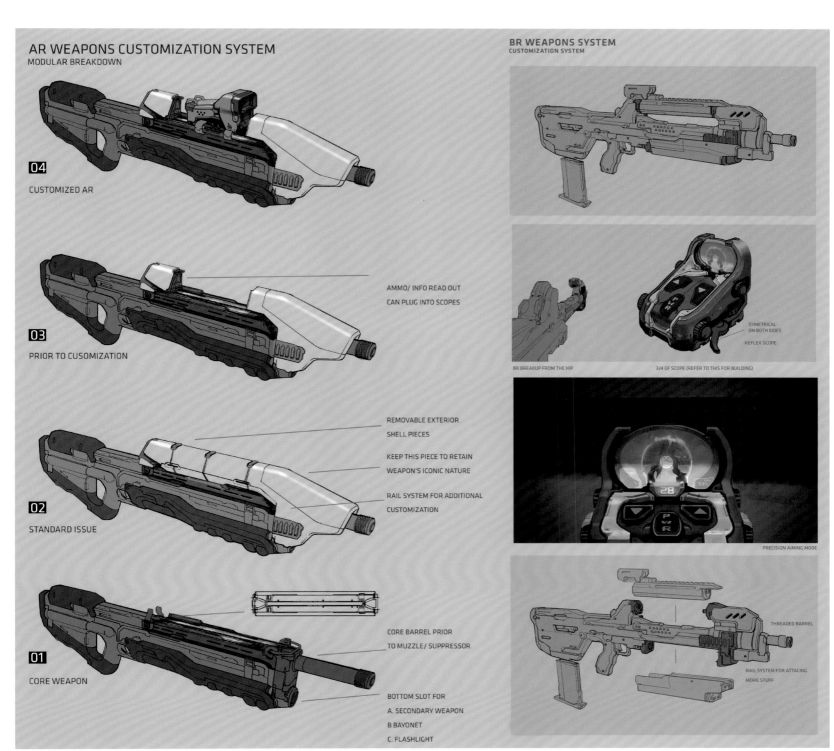

AR WEAPONS CUSTOMIZATION SYSTEM
MODULAR BREAKDOWN

04
CUSTOMIZED AR

03
PRIOR TO CUSOMIZATION

AMMO/ INFO READ OUT
CAN PLUG INTO SCOPES

REMOVABLE EXTERIOR
SHELL PIECES

KEEP THIS PIECE TO RETAIN
WEAPON'S ICONIC NATURE

RAIL SYSTEM FOR ADDITIONAL
CUSTOMIZATION

02
STANDARD ISSUE

01
CORE WEAPON

CORE BARREL PRIOR
TO MUZZLE/ SUPPRESSOR

BOTTOM SLOT FOR
A. SECONDARY WEAPON
B BAYONET
C. FLASHLIGHT

BR WEAPONS SYSTEM
CUSTOMIZATION SYSTEM

SYMETRICAL
ON BOTH SIDES

REFLEX SCOPE

BR BREAKUP FROM THE HIP

3/4 OF SCOPE (REFER TO THIS FOR BUILDING)

PRECISION AIMING MODE

THREADED BARREL

RAIL SYSTEM FOR ATTACING
MORE STUFF

Shae Shatz

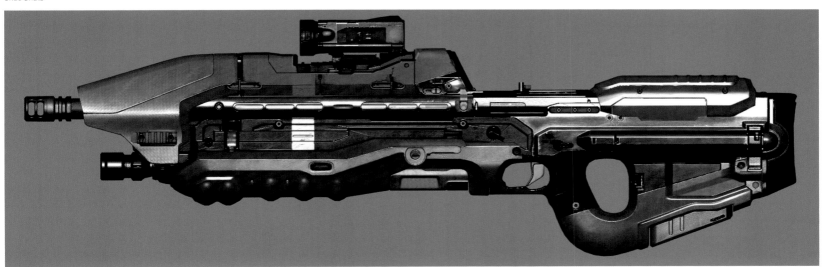

Sparth

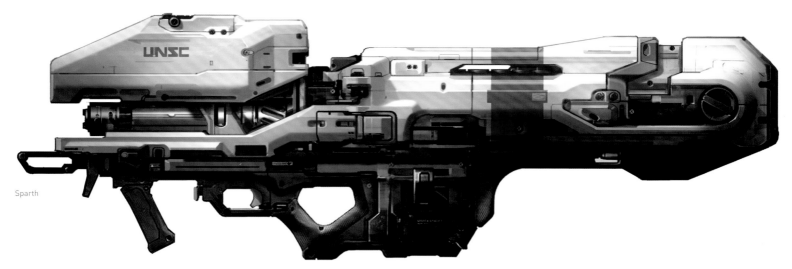

Sparth

Sam Brown

Multiple Launch Rocket System (MLRS)

suitable screen this one can be transparent, or just a simple framing structure (TBD)

radar system

reloading area

mecanism pushing ammo into barrel (TBD)

canon (there's only one)

rotating barrel

rotating engine area, powers the front barrel. it's a plus if we show some rotating features here.

Sparth

Sean Binder, Kolby Jukes, and Can Tuncer

152

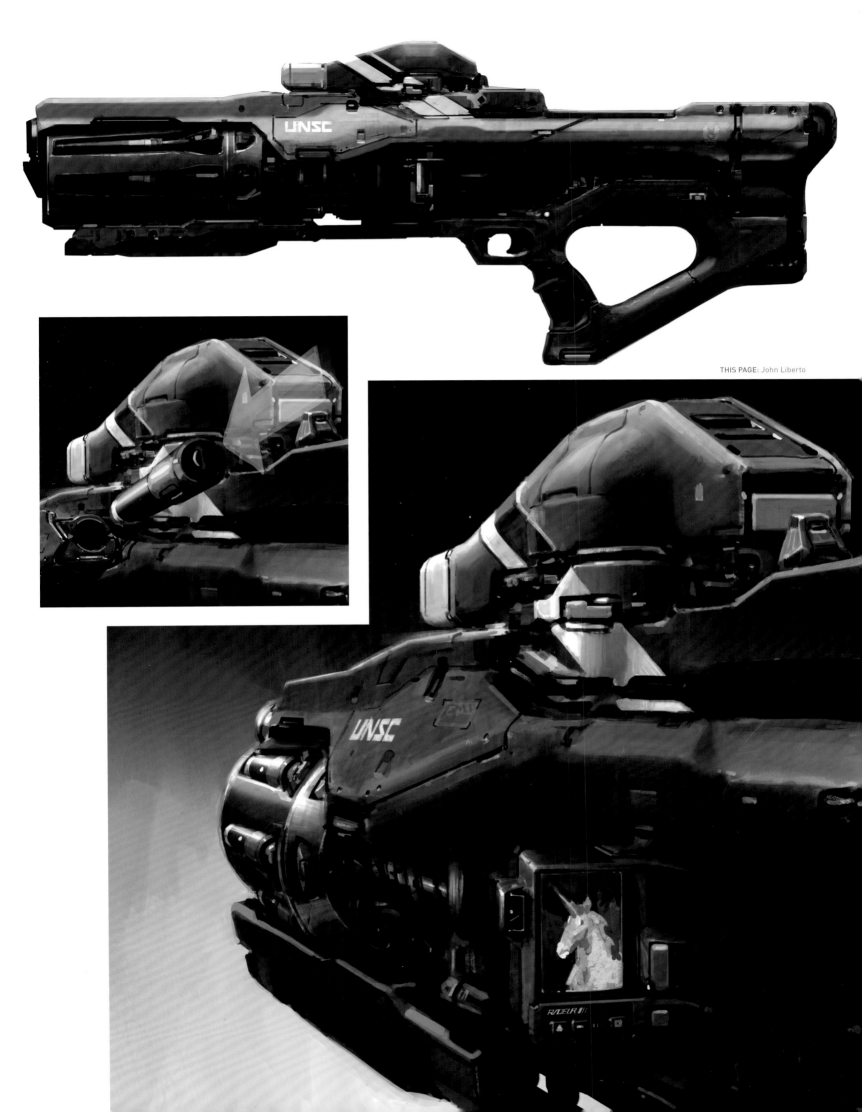

THIS PAGE: John Liberto

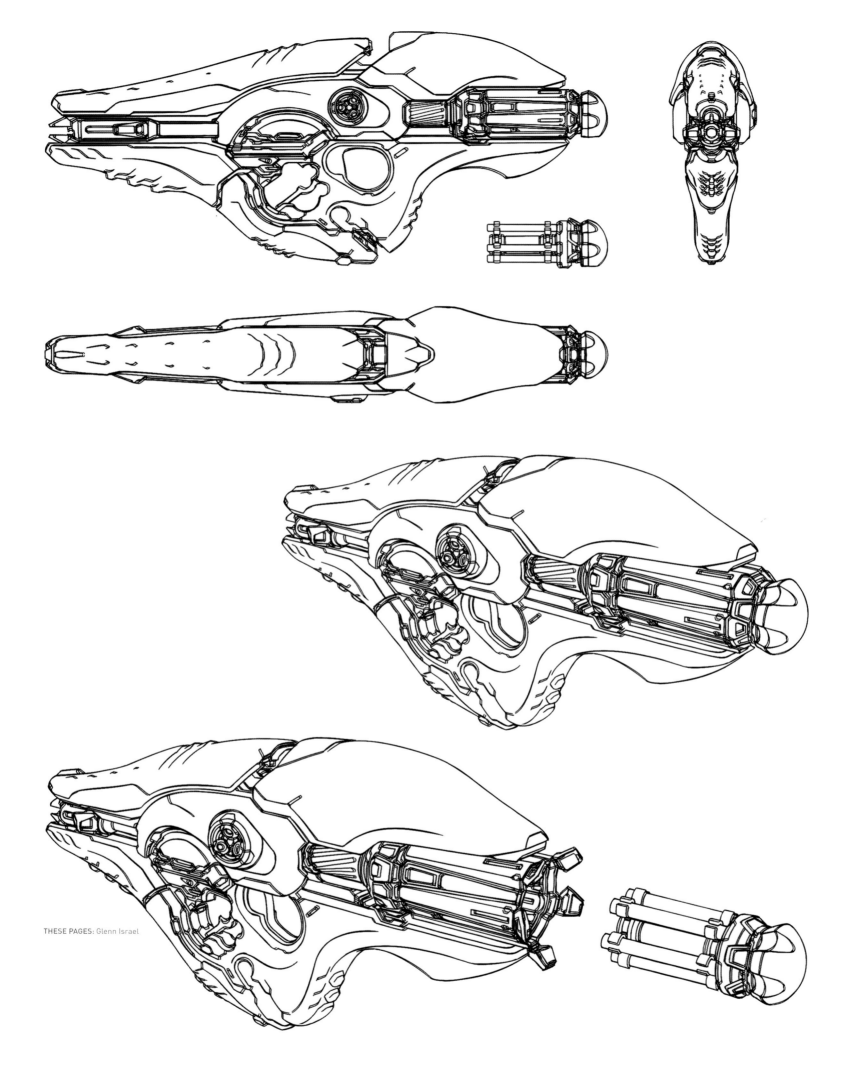

THESE PAGES: Glenn Israel

COVENANT WEAPONS

Before the discovery of Forerunner Promethean weapons, Covenant arms were considered some of the deadliest in the galaxy.

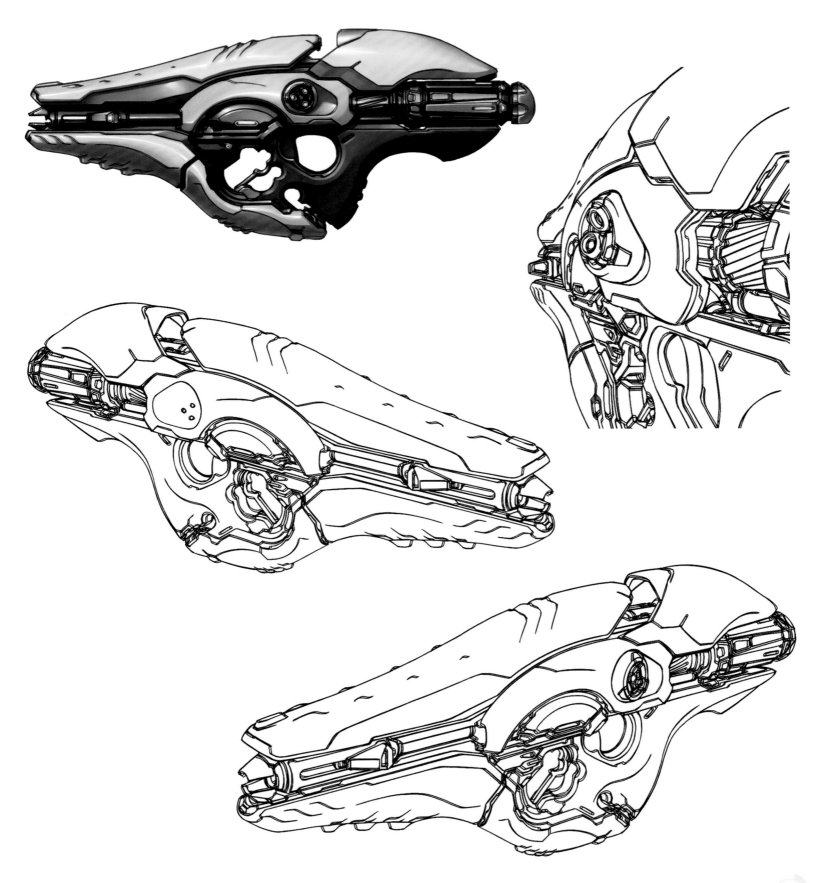

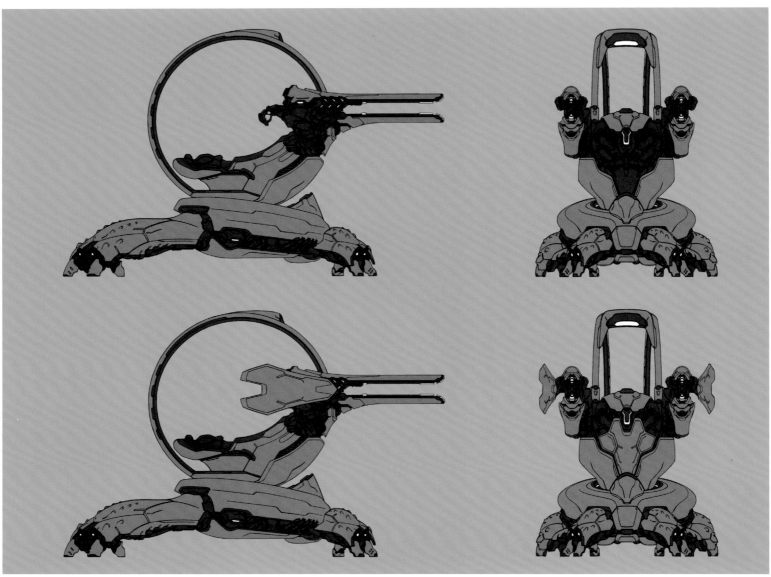

THIS PAGE: Glenn Israel

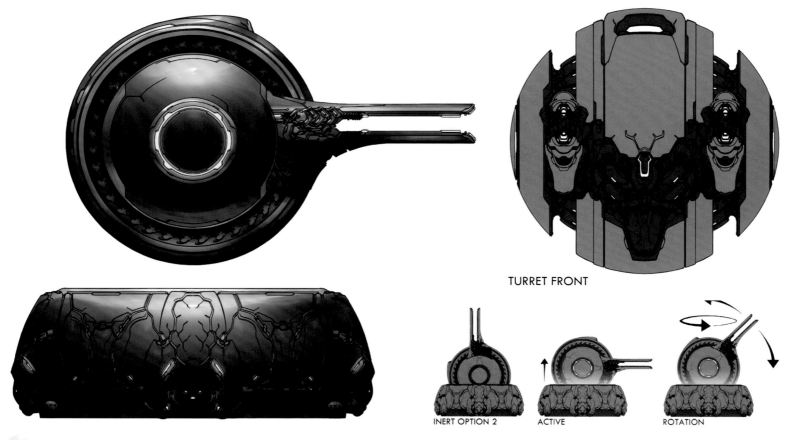

TURRET FRONT

INERT OPTION 2   ACTIVE   ROTATION

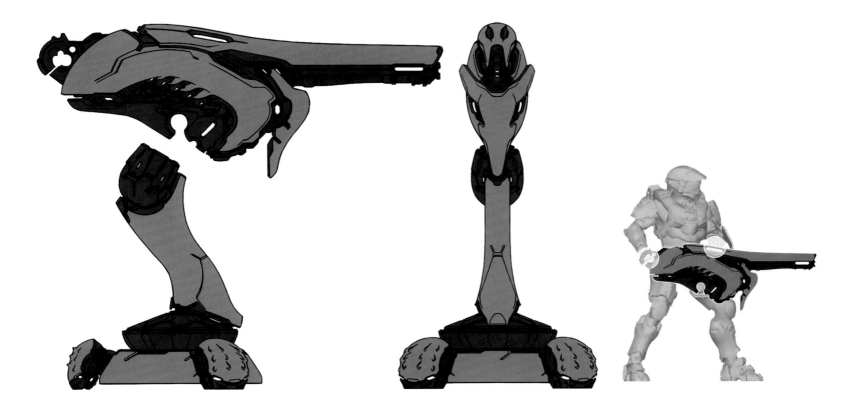

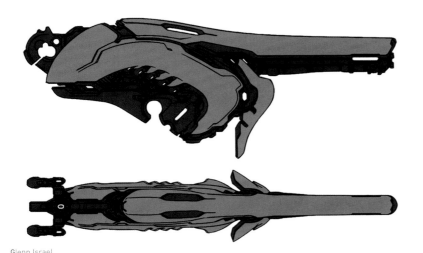

Glenn Israel

"For a long time we've played with the idea that Covenant technology is, to some degree or another, derived from Forerunner technology. They're adapting these technological marvels that they worship and then growing a skin or a shell around it as a way to preserve it and adapt it to their own purposes." —*Glenn Israel*

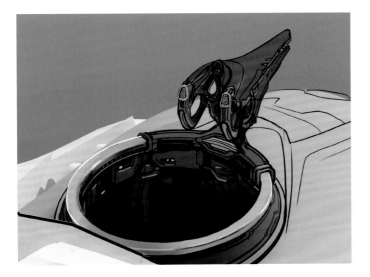

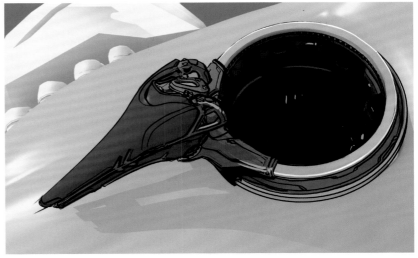

Alex Cunningham

"The Needler is a fan favorite. It's a weapon that has undergone a lot of changes over the years but always maintains the signature silhouette and the needles themselves; those have to be a central part of the design." —*Glenn Israel*

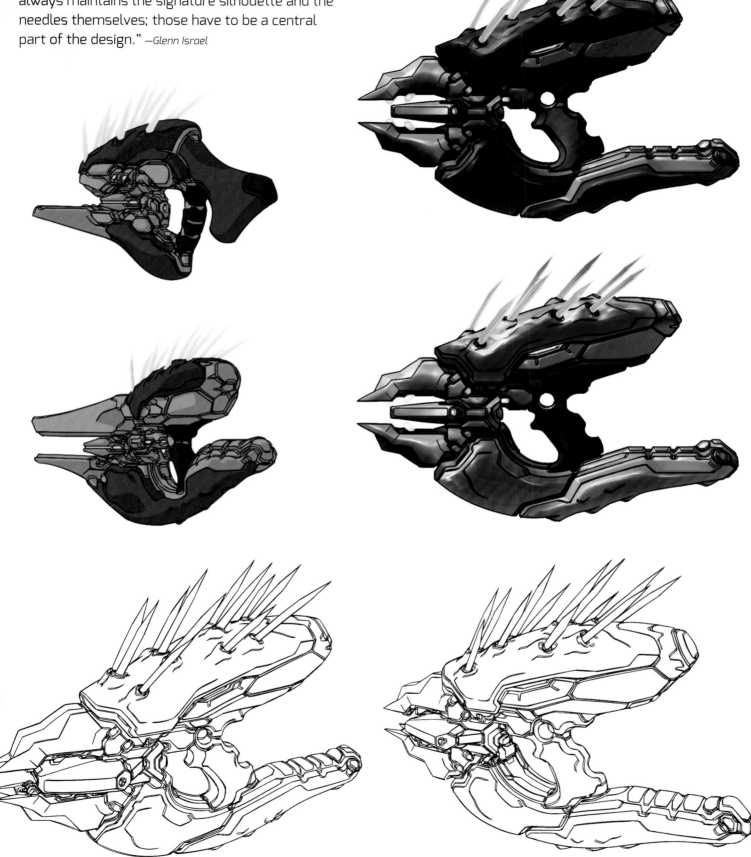

THESE PAGES: Glenn Israel

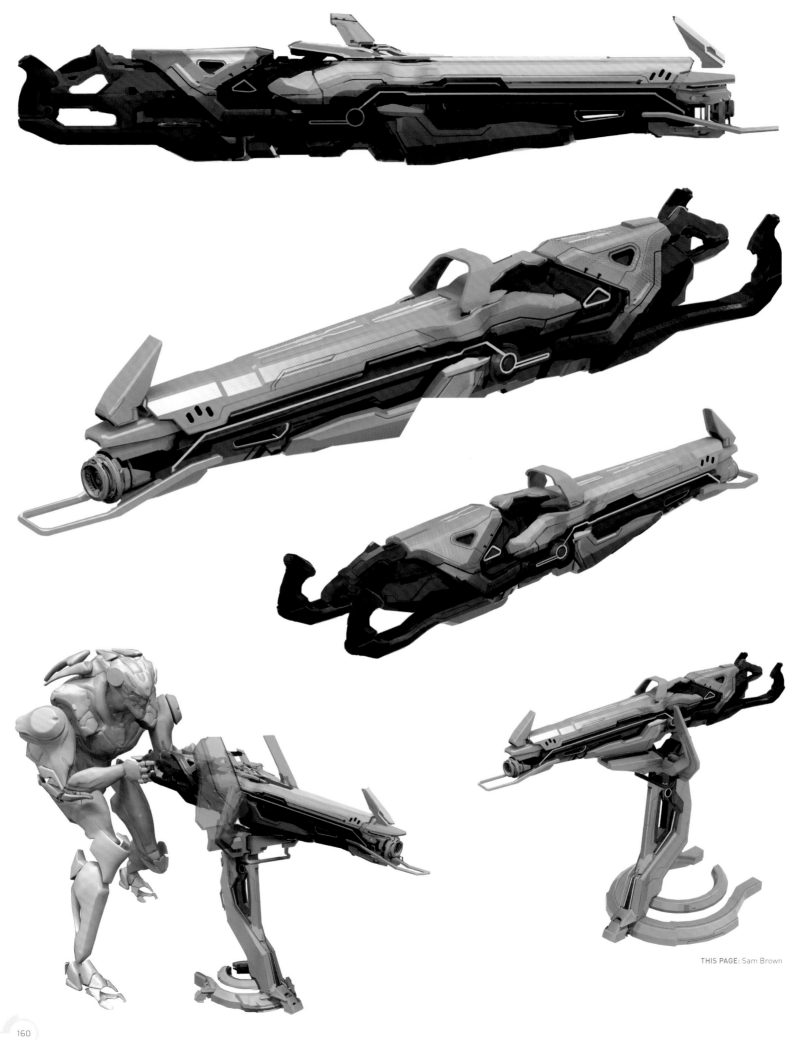

THIS PAGE: Sam Brown

FORERUNNER WEAPONS

First discovered by humanity on the shield world Requiem, the Forerunner's Promethean weapons are more advanced than anything we have seen before.

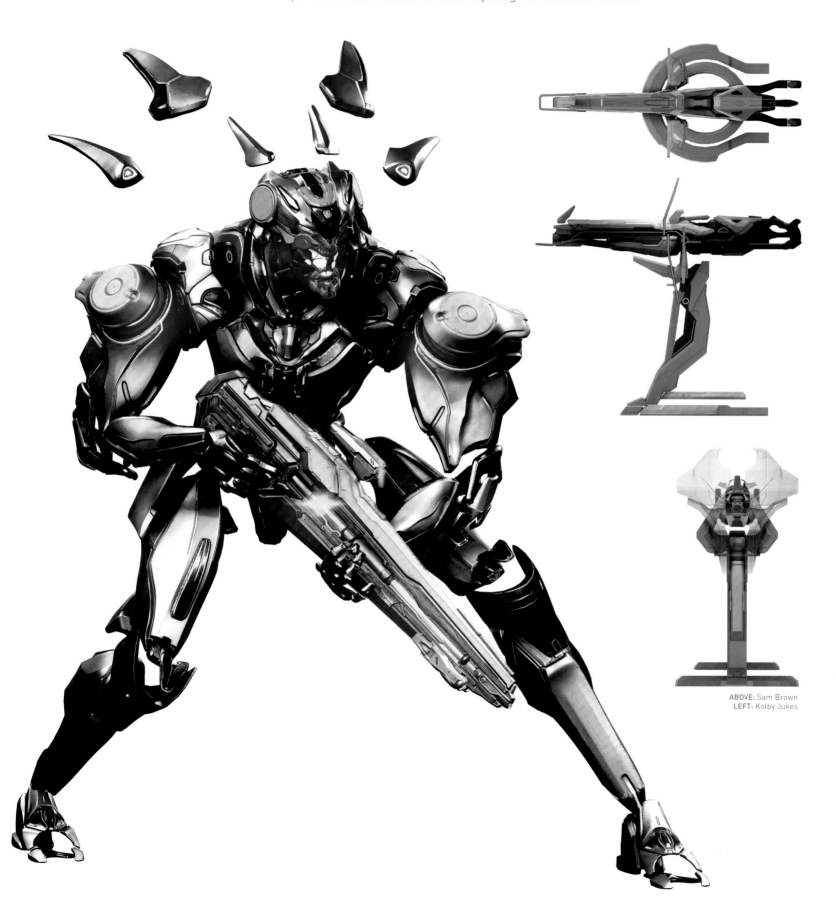

ABOVE: Sam Brown
LEFT: Kolby Jukes

John Liberto

04 VEHICLES

John Liberto

VEHICLE DESIGN

Successful hard surface design is all about believability, nailing design basics, and subtlety. Tiered above that, designing vehicles presents further challenges and unique complexities that we as designers are aware of when undertaking a task like expanding on an existing Halo design or creating a new one altogether. Viewers are told subconsciously via a vehicle's design expressions and subtleties how one should perceive the object based on design cues passed from the artist's hand to the player. In game creation, we as aesthetic designers must be conscious and careful of these subtle cues that are what set apart the great designs from the good, while also respecting the needs and uses for which the vehicle will be called upon in game. Penning our Halo vehicles with tight control over nuances of scale, details, and shape language, we strive to push functionality and selective realism in an attempt to make the end result as plausible (and cool) as possible. —Darren Bacon

Alex Cunningham

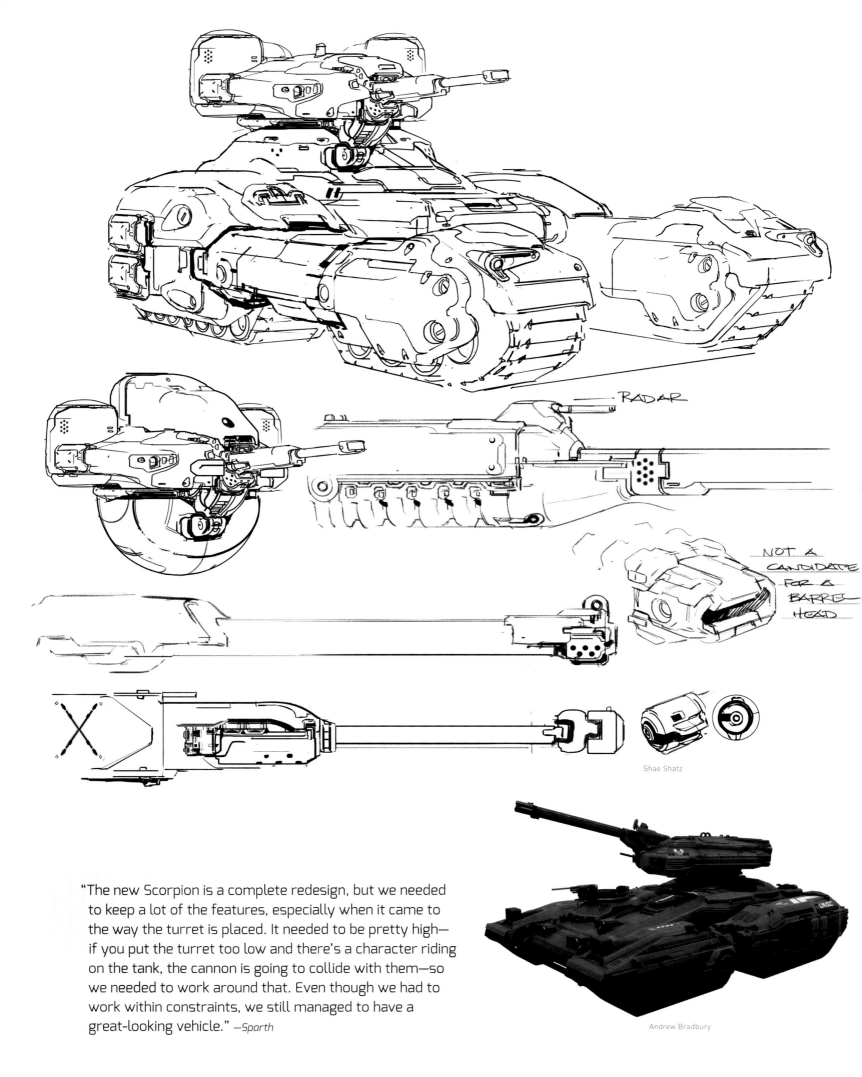

RADAR

NOT A
CANDIDATE
FOR A
BARREL
HEAD

Shae Shatz

"The new Scorpion is a complete redesign, but we needed to keep a lot of the features, especially when it came to the way the turret is placed. It needed to be pretty high—if you put the turret too low and there's a character riding on the tank, the cannon is going to collide with them—so we needed to work around that. Even though we had to work within constraints, we still managed to have a great-looking vehicle." —*Sparth*

Andrew Bradbury

UNSC VEHICLES

The finest engineering in human history makes it possible to explore the galaxy,
no matter the conditions.

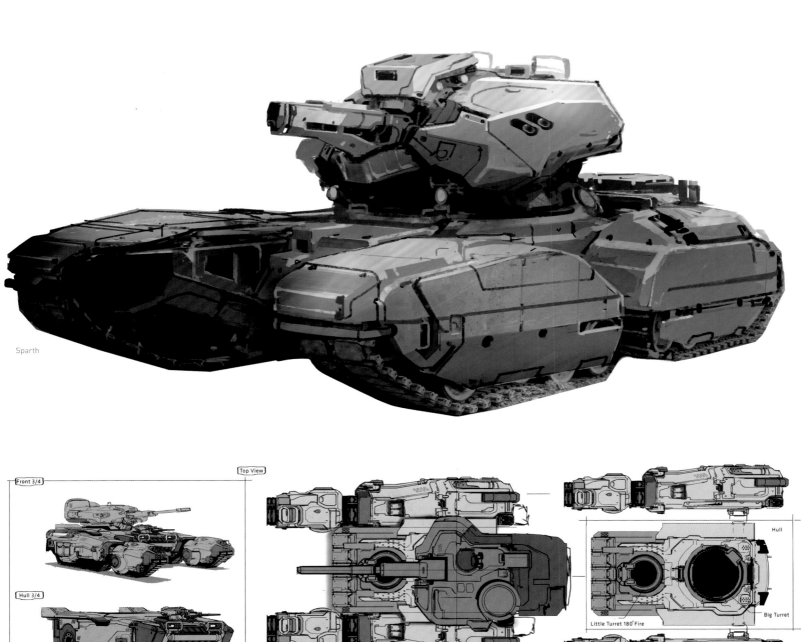

Sparth

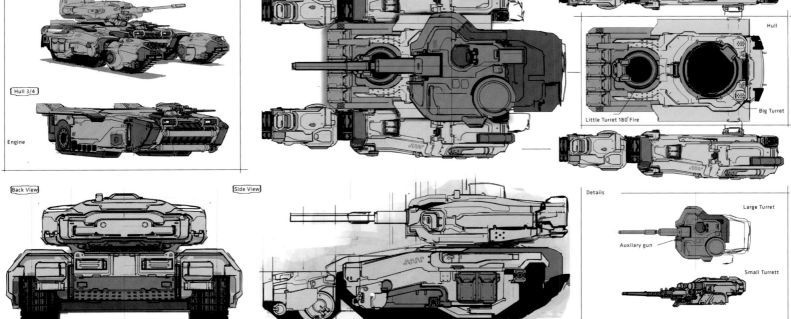

Shae Shatz

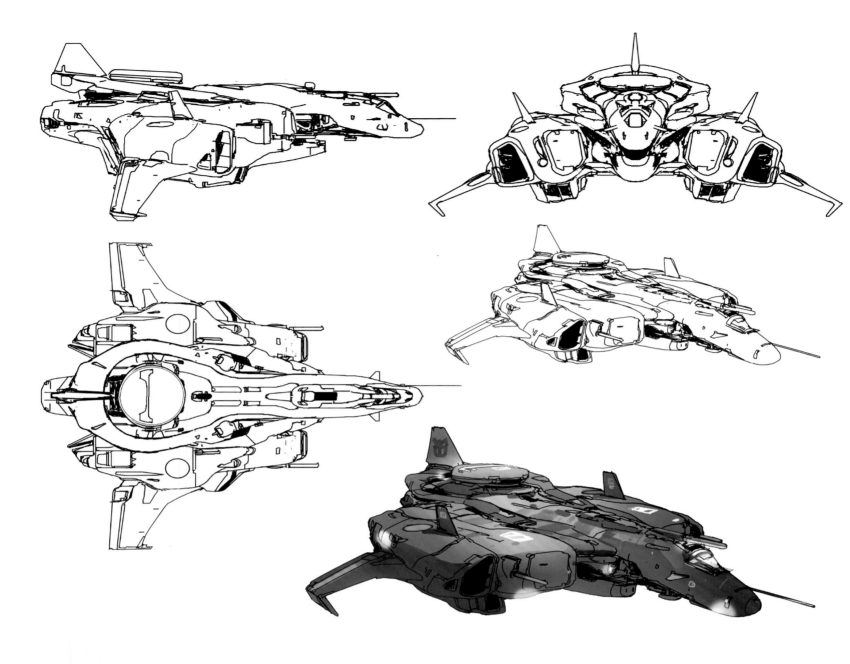

"The Prowler is secretive. It's very undercover, undetectable, stealth. In *Halo 5: Guardians* it became a larger vehicle with a few intricately connected features that are not a part of gameplay. So it looks really good. As an artist you have a little more freedom when something is there only for cinematic purposes!" —*Sparth*

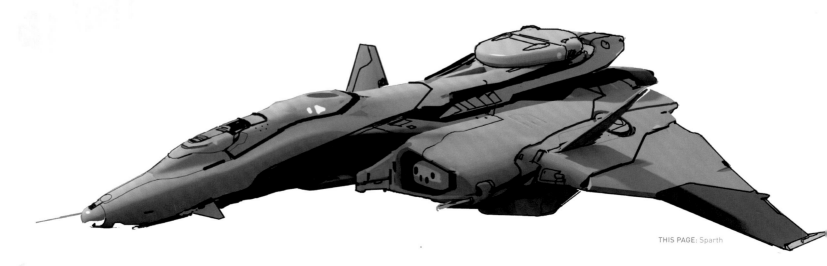

THIS PAGE: Sparth

John Liberto

Robogabo

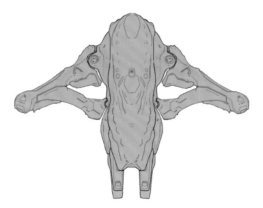

"These are classic designs, but we also wanted to further push the idea that this is tech that the Covenant inherited and adapted in their own way by growing the shell around it and adding all the little details, like muscular curves and bumps on the surface, as well as little knobs, protrusions, and spines. Those touches are very subtle, but for the player who looks deeper, it enriches the world." —Glenn Israel

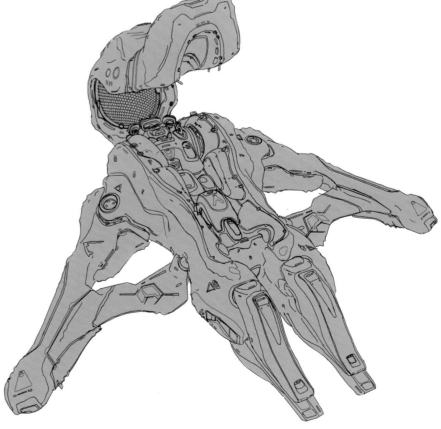

COVENANT VEHICLES

The Covenant's strength has long come from not just their fleet, but also their deadly ground and air forces.

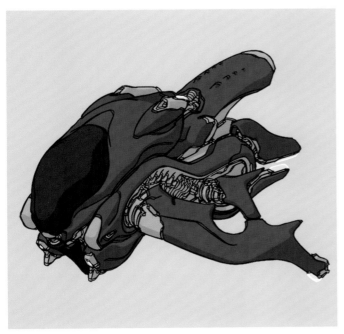

Glenn Israel

John Liberto

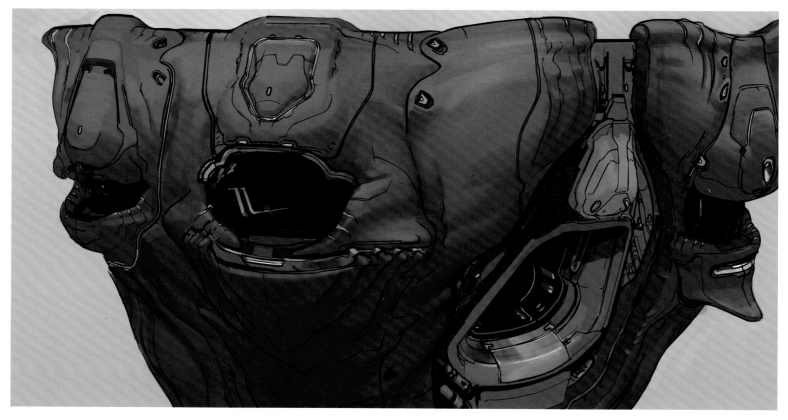

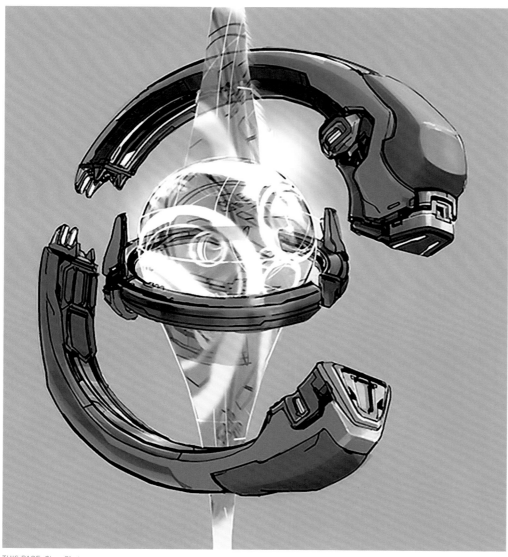

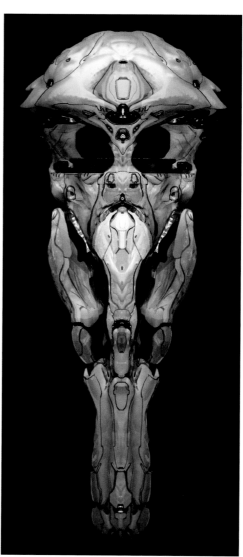

THIS PAGE: Shae Shatz

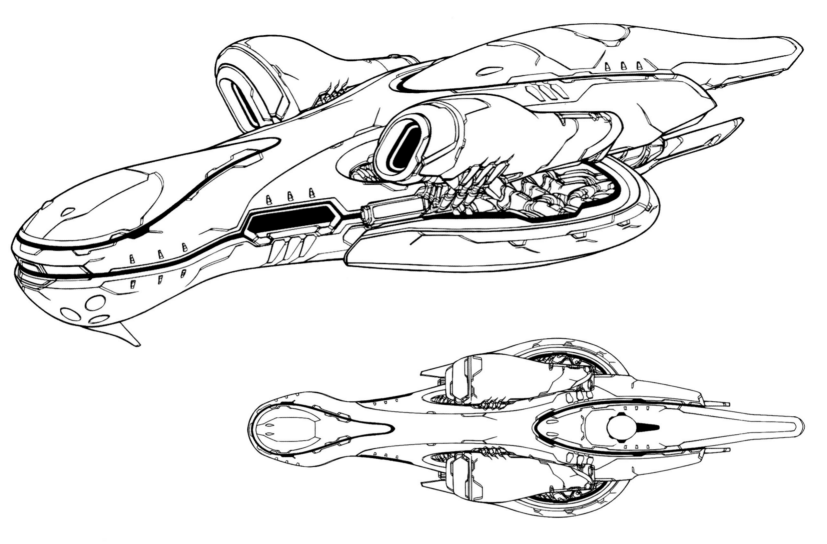

"The Covenant Wraith has been totally redesigned from scratch, and it's pretty amazing. It's 100 percent *Halo 5: Guardians*. The redesigns were to make sure that all Covenant vehicles have the same design feel as the fleet." —*Sparth*

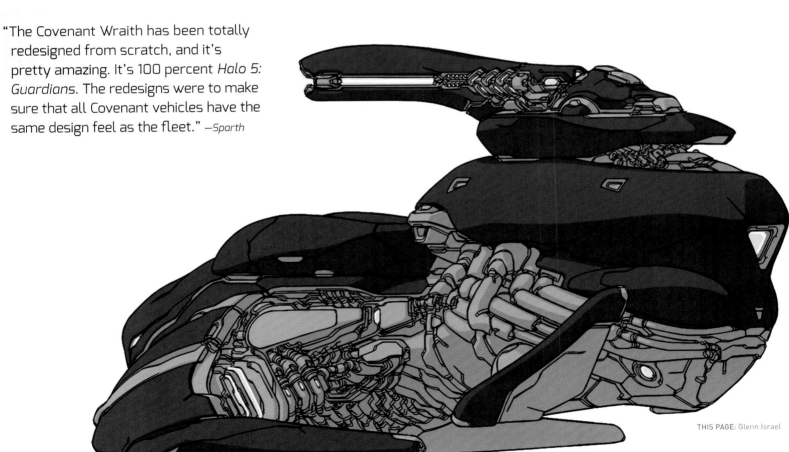

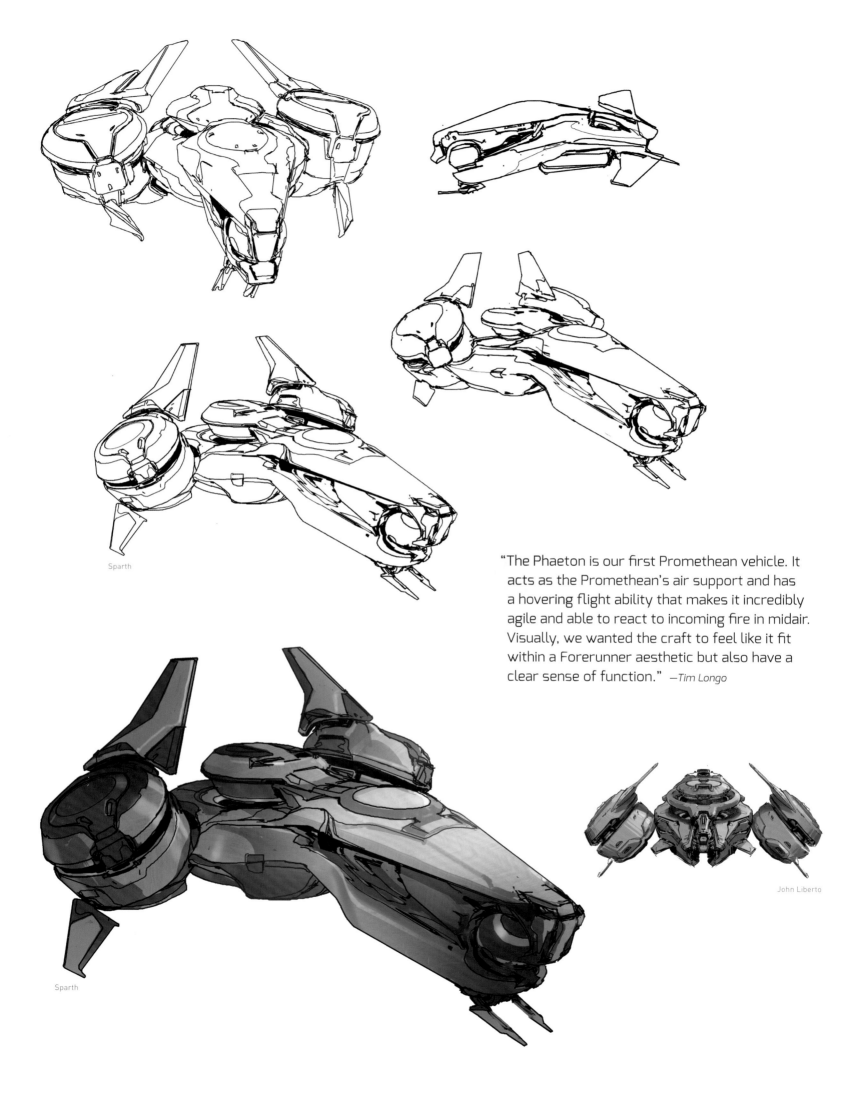

Sparth

"The Phaeton is our first Promethean vehicle. It acts as the Promethean's air support and has a hovering flight ability that makes it incredibly agile and able to react to incoming fire in midair. Visually, we wanted the craft to feel like it fit within a Forerunner aesthetic but also have a clear sense of function." —Tim Longo

Sparth

John Liberto

FORERUNNER VEHICLES

Little is known about Forerunner military vehicles, as so few have yet been encountered in the field.

THIS PAGE: John Liberto

John Liberto

06 WAR GAMES

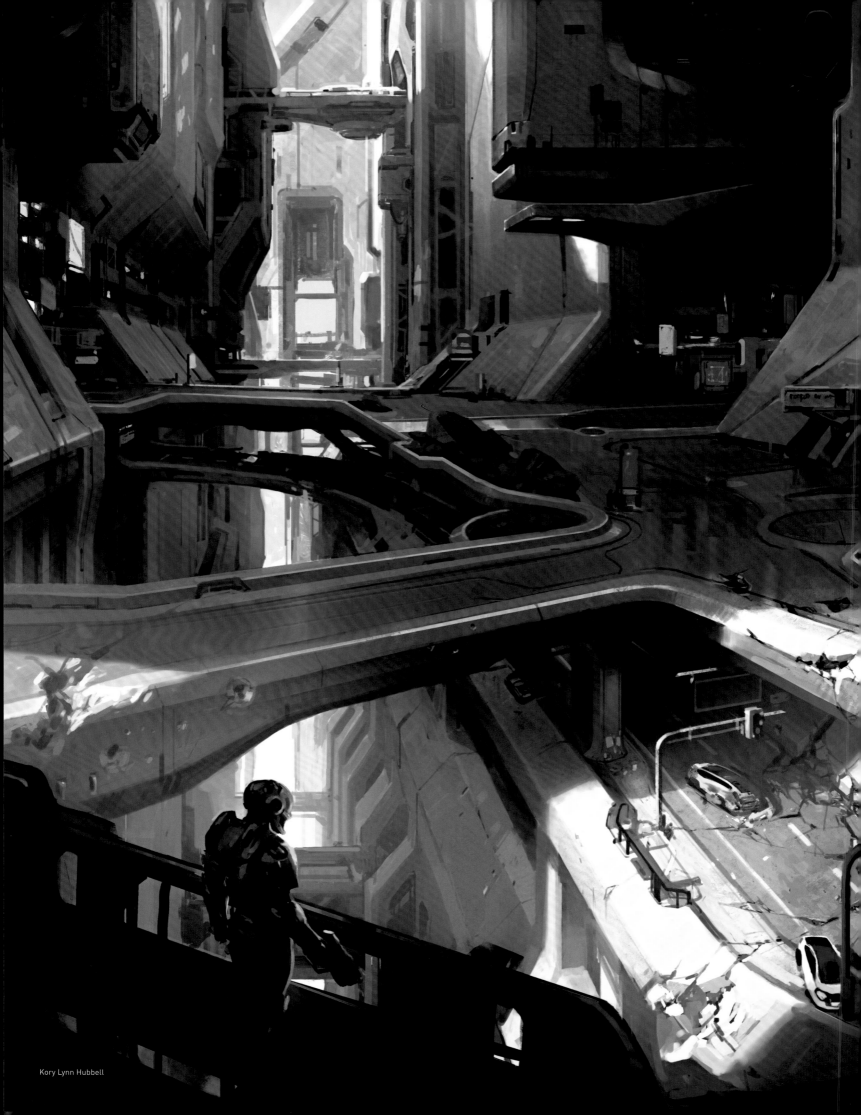

Kory Lynn Hubbell

DESIGNING ARENA AND WARZONE

For *Halo 5: Guardians*, game design has changed drastically because of the increased emphasis on co-op elements. It means that de facto level design is going to change, because a lot of these spaces are planned in advance to receive multiple characters playing together, meaning that you have larger hallways and larger spaces in order to be sure that the gameplay experience between characters is going to unfold in the best possible way. —Sparth

Gustavo Mendonca

Kenneth Scott

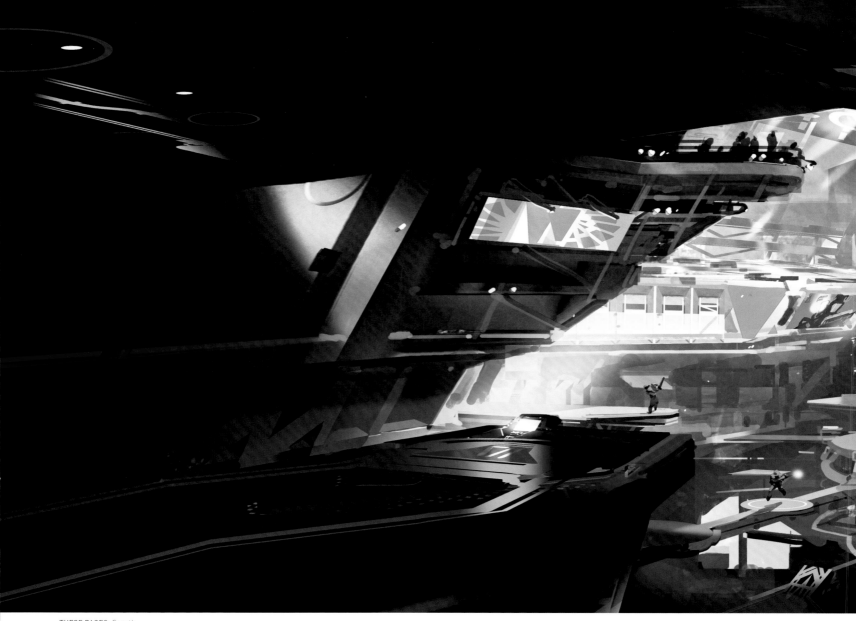

ARENA

Spartans train in the War Games simulator on board the UNSC *Infinity*.
The Arena, a small 4-versus-4 scenario, is more game than training regimen.
As such, it has become a form of entertainment for the crew.

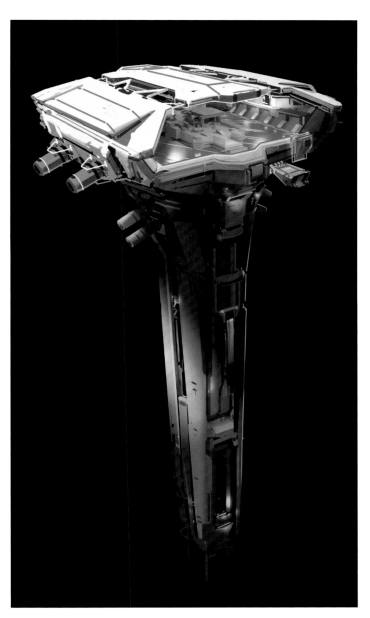

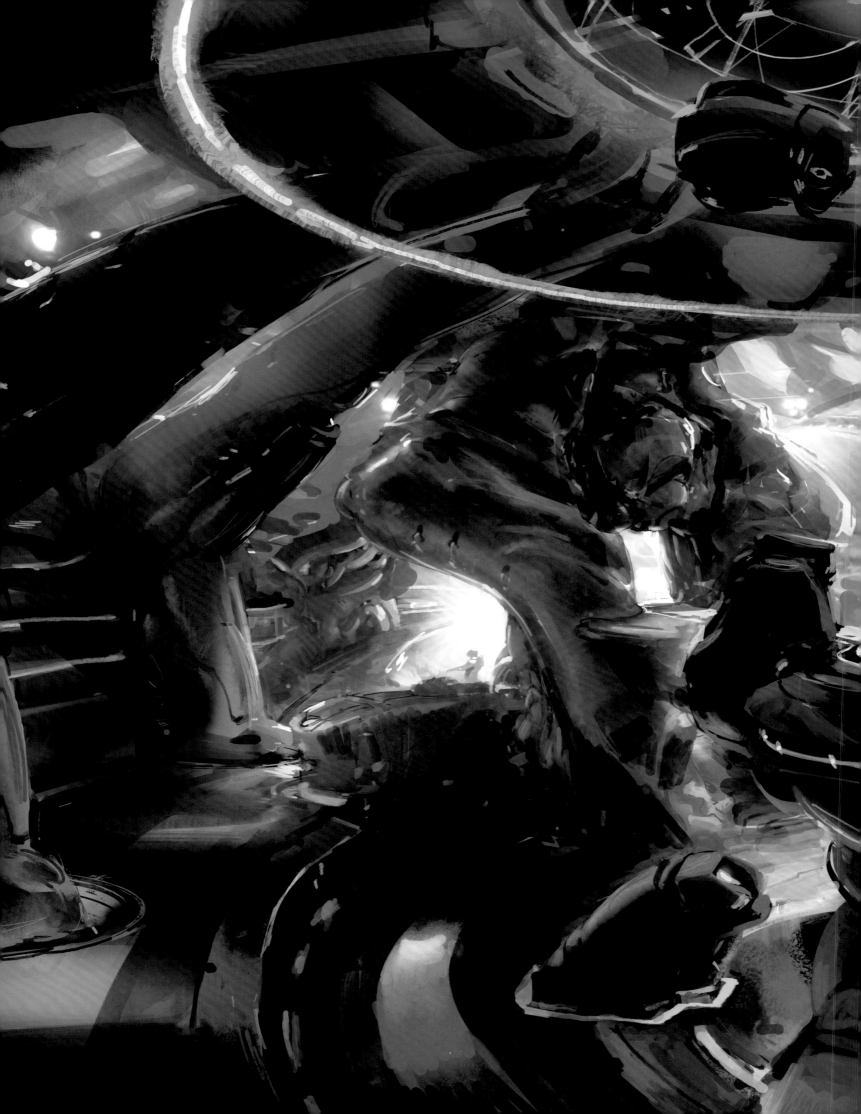

Sparth and John Liberto

Sparth

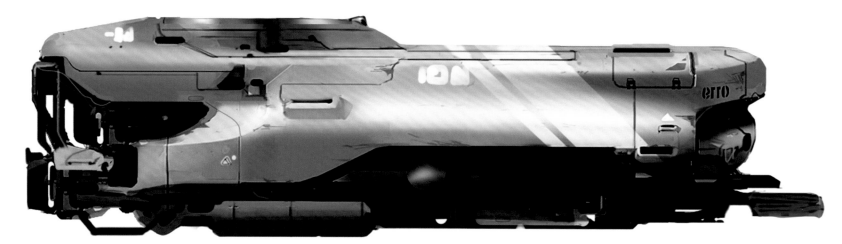

David Bolton and Sparth

Darren Bacon

ABOVE AND BELOW: Sparth

THIS PAGE: Sparth

Shae Shatz

Gustavo Mendonca

"The Arena is meant to open up the fighting experience. When you look at the Arena maps that we have, it's more like the highly technical levels for pro-gamers, and it encourages a very specific and intense type of gameplay." —*Sparth*

Justin Oaksford

Sparth

Justin Oaksford

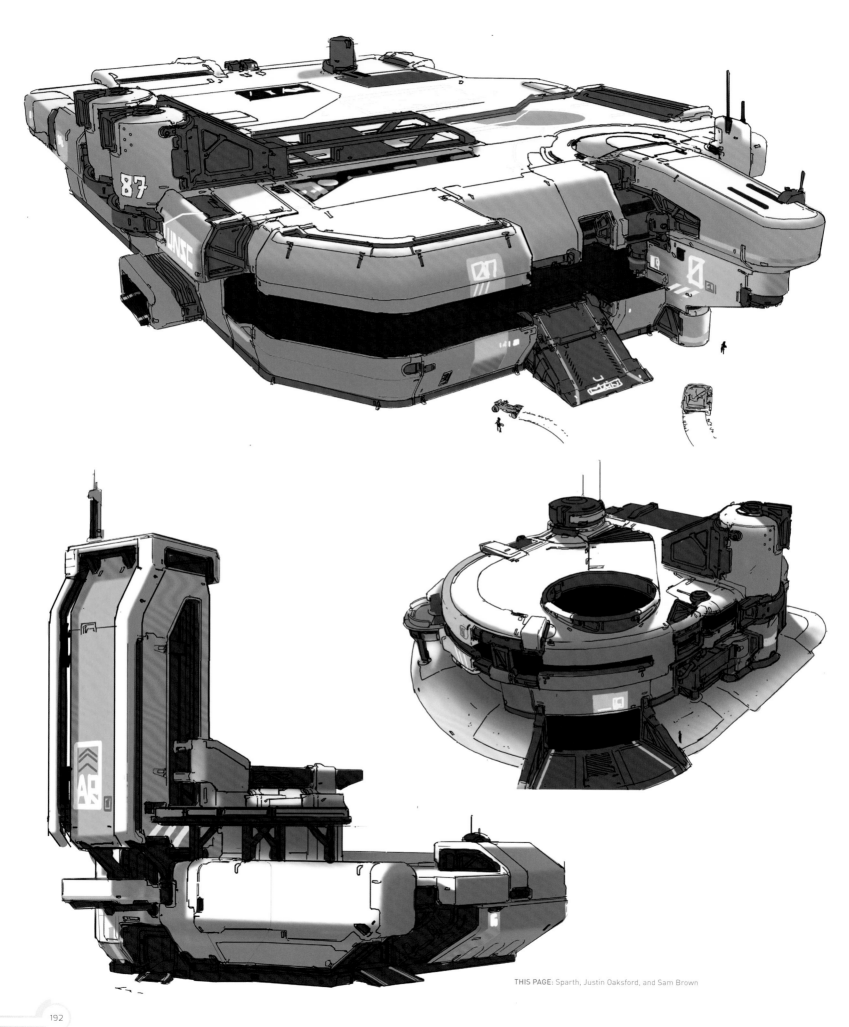

THIS PAGE: Sparth, Justin Oaksford, and Sam Brown

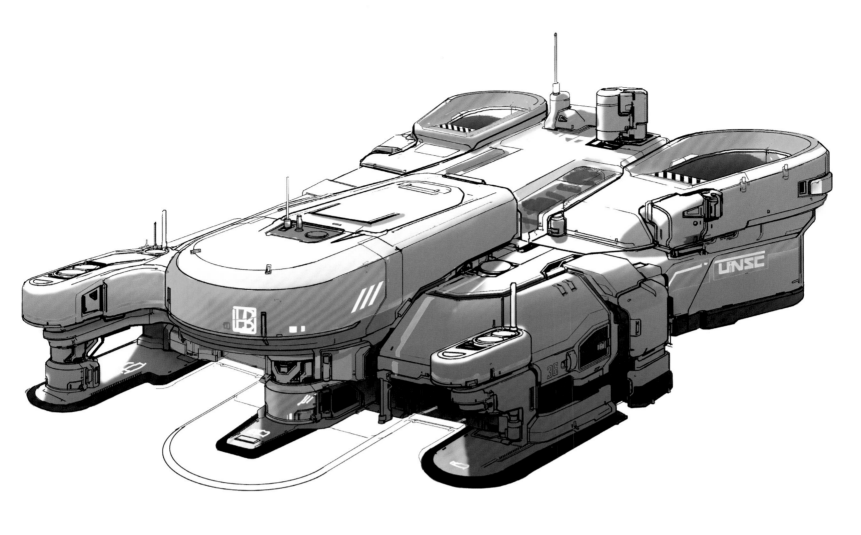

ABOVE: Sparth, Justin Oaksford, and Sam Brown
BELOW: Sam Brown

Justin Oaksford

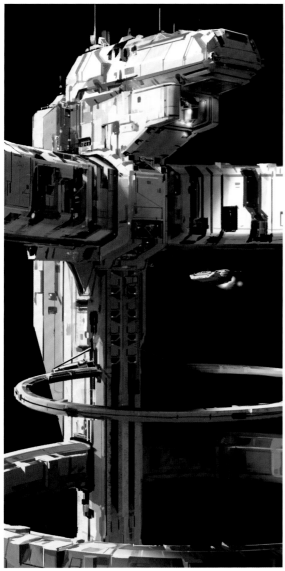

Sparth

Sparth

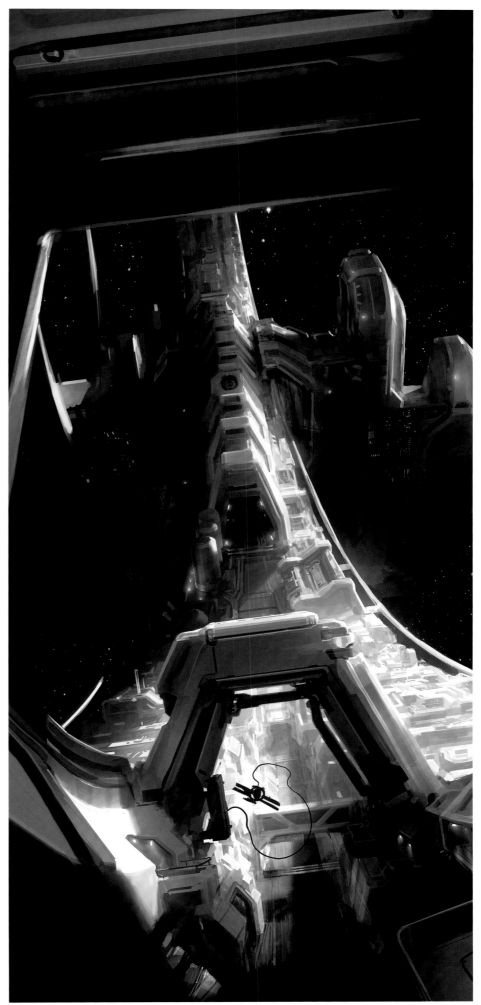

Justin Oaksford

Sparth

WARZONE

A key piece of the War Games training facility, the Warzone is a means for Spartans and other military forces to safely practice combined-arms tactics.

Sparth

Kory Lynn Hubbell

Sparth

"Warzone is the biggest Halo experience to date. It is the best aspects of Halo combined into one mode. Warzone has objective-based multiplayer combat, vehicles, enemy AI within the battlefield, and even bosses to hunt down. Warzone is also a 24-player game mode, so the raging battles are bigger than ever before on the largest Halo maps to date." —*Tim Longo*

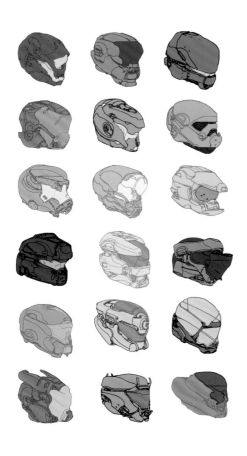

"For the armor skins, it's important to keep the primary color the largest proportion of color but use the secondary color to add something that looks customizable to the armor." —Sam Brown

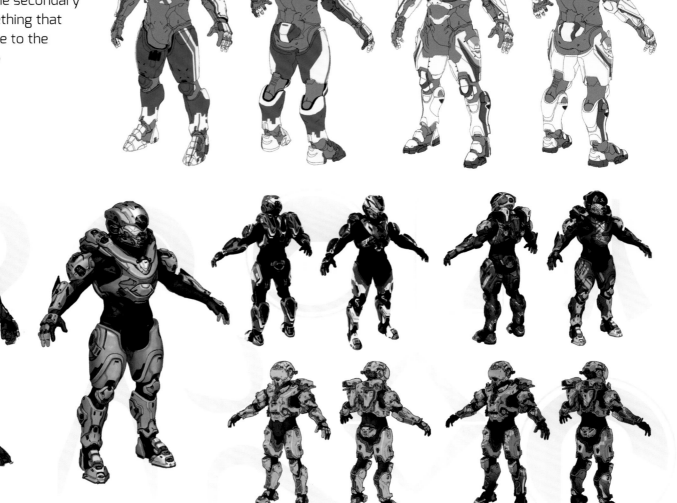

THESE PAGES: David Bolton, Sam Brown, Daniel Chavez, Alex Cunningham, Kory Lynn Hubbell, Paul Richards, and Janet Ung

ARMORS

Even though Spartan IVs have a wide range of powered assault armors available for use, most settle on a personal style early in their career and stick to it.

WEAPONS SKINS

A recent trend in War Games matches is for Spartan IVs to customize their weapons with a personal flair. While not strictly adhering to UNSC guidelines, these "skins" harken back to the personalization of armor and weapons exhibited by some Spartan IIs.

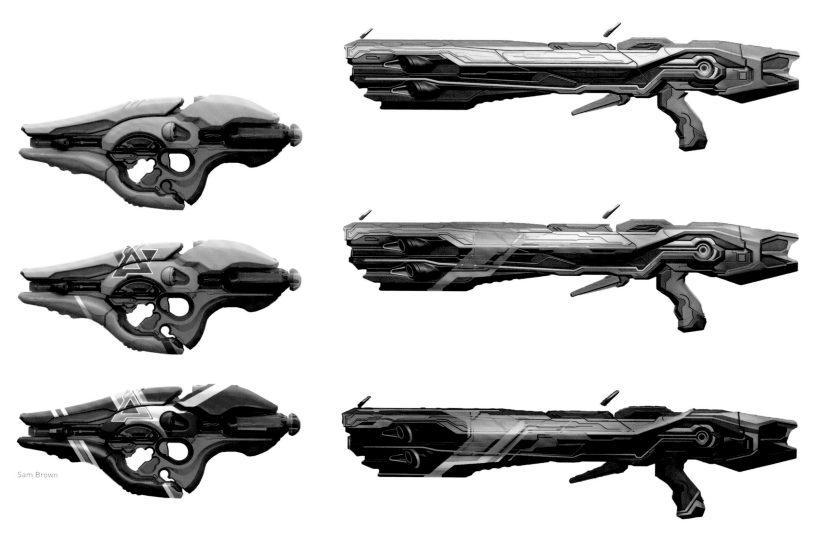

Sam Brown

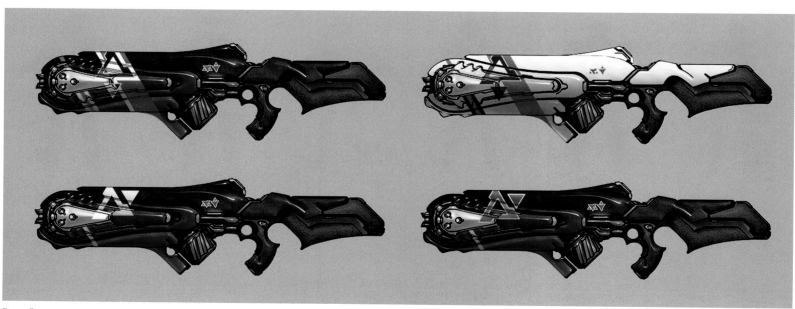

Darren Bacon

Justin Oaksford

Sam Brown

John Liberto

Justin Oaksford

INSIGHT EDITIONS

PO Box 3088
San Rafael, CA 94912
www.insighteditions.com

 Find us on Facebook: www.facebook.com/InsightEditions

 Follow us on Twitter: @insighteditions

Published by Insight Editions, San Rafael, California, in 2015. No part of this book may be reproduced in any form without written permission from the publisher.

Library of Congress Cataloging-in-Publication Data available.
ISBN: 978-1-60887-649-5

Publisher: Raoul Goff
Acquisitions Manager: Robbie Schmidt
Art Director: Chrissy Kwasnik
Designer: Chris Kosek
Executive Editor: Vanessa Lopez
Senior Editor: Dustin Jones
Editorial Assistant: Katie DeSandro
Production Editor: Elaine Ou
Production Manager: Anna Wan

 ROOTS of PEACE   ⊕ REPLANTED PAPER

Insight Editions, in association with Roots of Peace, will plant two trees for each tree used in the manufacturing of this book. Roots of Peace is an internationally renowned humanitarian organization dedicated to eradicating land mines worldwide and converting war-torn lands into productive farms and wildlife habitats. Roots of Peace will plant two million fruit and nut trees in Afghanistan and provide farmers there with the skills and support necessary for sustainable land use.

Manufactured in Hong Kong by Insight Editions

10 9 8 7 6 5 4 3 2 1

343 INDUSTRIES WOULD LIKE TO THANK Bungie Studios, Scott Dell'Osso, Christine Finch, John Friend, Josh Holmes, Dustin Jones, Bryan Koski, Tim Longo, Vanessa Lopez, Matt McCloskey, Bonnie Ross-Ziegler, Rob Semsey, Matt Skelton, Phil Spencer, Carla Woo, and Jennifer Yi.

Additional thanks to the 343 staff who helped put this book together: Darren Bacon, Kyle Hunter, Tyler Jeffers, Scott Jobe, Carlos Naranjo, Tiffany O'Brien, Frank O'Connor, Jeremy Patenaude, Kenneth Peters, Brian Reed, Corrinne Robinson, Nahil Sharkasi, Sparth, and Kiki Wolfkill.

ACKNOWLEDGEMENTS

There is an exceptional amount of work that is done before the artists even begin. We would like to give special thanks to the behind-the-scenes talent without whom this book would not be possible.

Matt Aldridge
Darren Bacon
Sean Binder
David Bolton
Nicolas "Sparth" Bouvier
Andrew Bradbury
Sam Brown
Daniel Chavez
Alex Cunningham
Stephen Dyck
Gabriel "Robogabo" Garza
Brien Goodrich
Gareth Hector (Axis)
Kyle Hefley
David Heidhoff
Kory Lynn Hubbell
Glenn Israel

Kolby Jukes
Josh Kao
Jihoon Kim
Peter Konig
John Wallin Liberto
Gustavo Mendonca
Albert Ng
Justin Oaksford
Paul Richards
Dan Sarkar
Kenneth Scott
Shae Shatz
Can Tuncer
Janet Ung
Eric Will
Jaemus Wurzbach